CRITICAL ISSUES IN EDUCATIONAL LEADERSHIP SERIES

Joseph Murphy, Series Editor

Cognitive Perspectives on Educational Leadership
Philip Hallinger, Kenneth Leithwood, and Joseph Murphy, Editors

Reclaiming Educational Administration as a Caring Profession
Lynn G. Beck

Reclaiming
Educational Administration
as a
Caring Profession

LYNN G. BECK

Foreword by Nel Noddings

Teachers College, Columbia University
New York and London

Published by Teachers College Press, 1234 Amsterdam Avenue,
New York, NY 10027

Library of Congress Cataloging-in-Publication Data

Beck, Lynn G.
    Reclaiming educational administration as a caring profession / Lynn G. Beck ;
foreword by Nel Noddings.
        p.   cm. — (Critical issues in educational leadership series)
    Includes bibliographical references and index.
    ISBN 0-8077-3314-8. — ISBN 0-8077-3313-X (pbk.)
    1. School management and organization—United States.   2. Caring.
    I. Title.   II. Series.
    LB2805.B348   1994
    371.2'00973—dc20   93-41848

ISBN 0-8077-3314-8
ISBN 0-8077-3313-X (pbk.)

Printed on acid-free paper
Manufactured in the United States of America

01 00 99 98 97 96 95 94   8 7 6 5 4 3 2 1

For

Sarah Barry, Lucy, and George Gillespie
and
Ann and Elizabeth O'Connell

In the hope that all of the educators in your
lives are caring

"Educational leaders must deal with loss all the time. The loss of academic standards. The loss of the common core curriculum. The loss of teacher authority, principal authority, school authority, parental authority. The loss of nonunionized angels of teaching virtue. The loss of households with school-age children. The loss of local control. The loss of middle- and upper-class student talent to private education. The loss of public and policymaker confidence in public education. The loss of safe schools free from the threat of mass murderers. The loss of children and youth to substance abuse, suicide, teenage parenthood, gangs, prisons, hotels for the homeless, and illiteracy."

· · ·

"A sense of belonging often is a very important factor in how and how well we deal with loss."

—Brad Mitchell
"Loss, Belonging, and Becoming:
Social Policy Themes for Children
and Schools"

"The biggest disease today is not leprosy or tuberculosis, but rather the feeling of being unwanted, uncared for, and deserted by everybody."

—Mother Teresa of Calcutta

Contents

Foreword

Lynn Beck, in this well-documented study, demonstrates the centrality of caring in educational administration. Through examination of a wide range of meanings and justifications for caring as a moral orientation, she reminds us of a trend in administration that has sometimes been actualized, but more often has lain latent as a promise yet to be kept.

Caring is not just an ideal for Beck. She shows how it can be employed in meeting the most difficult challenges of contemporary schooling: improving academic performance, battling social problems, and rethinking organizational strategies. Important as it is to face these challenges, it may be even more important to construe caring as an end in itself. Young people in our schools speak poignantly of their longing to be cared for and the perceived lack of care that characterizes not only our schools but the society at large. From Mother Teresa to James Comer, we hear repeated the cry of those for whom "nobody cares." Beck shows how much is lost when we ignore that cry.

Caring is, thus, both a means and an end. But, as a way of being in the world of educational administration, it also serves as a lens through which to study policy issues. It helps us to refocus our attention on clients and those over whom we hold power. The tendency in highly bureaucratized systems is to attend most diligently to those above us in the hierarchy; much of an administrator's time goes into compliance. When we evaluate our work through the perspective of caring, we experience a motivational shift toward those who need us and to whom we must now respond.

In her discussion of preparation for caring administrators, Beck outlines a lifetime of learning. No actual, time-bound, training program could possibly accomplish all she prescribes, but the prescription is good for us nonetheless. It points us to a lifetime of learning and reinforces the notion that many of us are now promoting: Caring implies competence. When we genuinely care, we want to do our very best to effect worthwhile results for the recipients of our care. This means that caring is more than an attitude, much more than a warm, cuddly feeling. It is an orientation of deep concern that carries us out of ourselves and into the lives, despairs, struggles, and hopes of others. To care is to respond, and to respond responsibly, we must continually strive for increased competence.

Finally, Beck reminds us that we cannot prepare caring administrators unless those who educate them also care. Preparation programs must be designed in a framework of caring. Caring, as the saying is repeated these days, "goes all the way down." We look in vain for a layer at which it begins or ends.

Nel Noddings
Lee L. Jacks Professor of Child Education
Stanford University

Introduction

In the wake of the reform movements of the 1980s, several scholars have begun to challenge educators to consider a different type of reform. David Purpel (1989), labeling issues of recent efforts as "minor" and "trivial," calls for a "reconceptualization of the schooling process" (p. 3) so that educators embrace and embody "social justice and compassion" (p. 121). Others (Bellah, Madsen, Sullivan, Swidler, & Tipton, 1985; Coegan & Raebeck, 1989; Giroux, 1988a, 1988b; Smith, 1990; Wilshire, 1990) have drawn similar conclusions, challenging fundamental assumptions underlying many educational efforts and calling for the development of "cooperation, integration, and caring" (Coegan & Raebeck, 1989, p. 96) in school settings.

Caring, as a critical component of human interaction, has been explored by people in a number of fields, including family policy (Hobbs, Dokecki, Hoover-Dempsey, Moroney, Shayne, & Weeks, 1984), social policy (Watson, 1980), social welfare (Morris, 1986), and social work (Imre, 1982). These authors urge academicians in their respective disciplines and practitioners in the helping professions to move toward "the creation and support of a competent and caring society" (Hobbs et al., 1984, p. 4).

A few scholars, including Barth (1990), the contributors to Brabeck's edited *Who Cares? Theory, Research, and Educational Implications of the Ethic of Care* (1989), Gilligan (1982), Noddings (1984, 1992), Sergiovanni (1992), and Starratt (1991), have issued a special call to educators to recognize and practice a caring ethic. Following in the footsteps of these authors, I focus on the importance and appropriateness of educational administrators' reclaiming their profession as one that allows and encourages caring in schools and other educational settings.

My interest in the moral dimensions of administrative thought and practice was aroused when I engaged in two separate research efforts. The first was an independent study conducted under the direction of Dr. Paul Dokecki (Beck, 1990) in which I examined ways of thinking about the interplay between people and their social structures. In this study, I examined three commonly held views about how and why persons come together in groups. In the first view, the goal of human interaction is maximizing the chances of individual success or achievement, usually defined in tangible, material, or monetary terms. Within this perspective, independence, autonomy, and self-expression are highly valued, and social actions are generally governed by competitive and contractual ethics. A second perspective holds that the smooth and effective operation of the group or social structure is a primary goal of human relationships. Those who hold this view value utility and equality of outcomes and prefer ethics that stress conformity and cooperation, even coerced cooperation. The third perspective contends that the most appropriate reason for the formation of social structures is the promotion of human or personal development within the context of communities. The dominant values of this perspective are fraternity and compassionate justice, and the major ethical systems revolve around caring and the building of community.

In the process of exploring these three viewpoints, I have come to believe that the third viewpoint offers the most hope for effecting a true transformation of schools. I am convinced that this perspective, with its attendant values and ethics, can be justified both philosophically and practically as being appropriate in the practice of educational administration. Furthermore, I believe that a conceptual framework that emphasizes personal development, the cultivation of community, and an ethic of caring, offers the only valid starting point from which academicians and practitioners can hammer out organizational and instructional theories and methodologies that can adequately meet the challenges facing education in the 1990s and beyond.

A second research effort, in which Dr. Joseph Murphy and I conducted a historical analysis of the metaphorical language used to discuss the role of the principal (Beck & Murphy, 1993), led me to a conclusion that further inspired this effort to call educational administrators to claim the right to operate from a perspective that embraces caring and community building. This conclusion, simply stated, is that educational theorists and administrators have often defined their purposes and professional roles in a reactive response to political and historical events or to social or cultural pressures rather than out of a proactive concern about the needs of students and teachers. I am convinced that it is both appropriate and necessary for educators to reclaim the right to define their goals and roles in schools and school systems and within the larger society. Furthermore, as noted in the preceding paragraph, I believe that this reclaiming, if it is to be truly effective in transforming education, must involve educators' exercising their right to create school structures and professional practices that are influenced by and conducive to an ethic of caring. This work is, thus, my effort to construct a framework that can guide academicians and practitioners in considering ways in which caring can and should influence educational endeavors.

The text is organized along the following lines: In Chapter 1, I attempt to clarify what I mean by "a caring ethic." Drawing from scholarship in a number of disciplines, I use broad strokes to paint a picture of caring. In Chapters 2 and 3, I focus on justifying the inclusion of a caring ethic in administration. Following Frankena (1973) and Strike, Haller, and Soltis (1988), I begin in Chapter 2 with nonconsequentialist or deontological arguments for caring in education. Then, I turn my attention in the third chapter to consequentialist teleological arguments. In Chapters 4 through 6, the focus shifts from the theoretical to the practical as I discuss changes that will need to occur if the transformative ethics of caring, concern, and compassionate justice are to become realities in education. In Chapter 4, I examine challenges that, according to leading scholars, currently face educational leaders, focusing specifically on the ways an ethic of caring might aid administrators and those charged with preparing them in meeting these challenges. Chapters 5 and 6 explore changes that need to occur in administrator practice and preparation; those chapters include a discussion of policies and practices that, in small pockets around this country, demonstrate ways a caring ethic can help to transform education. I conclude by offering thoughts about the urgency of the need for caring in our schools.

Worthy of note is a brief discussion of the ways in which I use the work of others to support my arguments and assertions. Throughout this work, I draw upon insights offered by persons representing a diverse set of disciplines and perspectives. In so doing, I am not suggesting that those I cite would agree entirely with me or with one another. Rather, I am attempting to show that caring—as a foundational ethic—addresses concerns and needs as expressed by *many* persons; that it, in a sense, transcends ideological boundaries; and that a commitment to care—especially for youngsters in our schools—may be able to provide a common focus around which we can come together and begin to build schools that are genuinely good, happy, healthy, and productive places.

1 Caring Defined

> . . . Words strain,
> Crack and sometimes break under the burden
> Under the tension, slips, slide, perish,
> Decay with imprecision, will not stay in place
> Will not stay still
> (T. S. Eliot, *The Four Quartets,* 1971, p. 121)

Caring is an elusive concept in that few people, especially those concerned with social science or social service, are against it and most believe that they practice it. Thus, caring becomes linked to a wide variety of attitudes and actions. T. S. Eliot, in the lines quoted above, was writing of the challenge to poets, but his words apply equally well to the challenge of defining an ethical practice such as caring. In this chapter, I attempt to respond to the imprecision of words by developing a definition that is: (1) systematic in that it organizes thoughts on caring into several categories; (2) comprehensive in that it considers several facets of caring both as an ethical imperative and as a practical activity; (3) precise in that it delineates goals, practices, and conditions related to caring; and (4) reflective in that it recognizes the thinking of scholars from a number of disciplines.

Two points are worthy of note before I offer this definition. The first relates to the language in this discussion. Various words will appear in this definition of caring—especially as I quote from other authors. For example, I will draw insights from Fromm's (1956) discussion of "loving," from Kirkpatrick's (1986) notes on "fellowship and communion," from McWilliams's (1973) work on "fraternity," and from Mitchell's (1990a) comments on "nurturance of belonging." I recognize that these words are not always exact synonyms for the concept being examined, but I and many authors I cite believe that they convey important ideas about the many dimensions of caring. The second relates to the sense in which I am using the word *caring*. Blustein (1991) and Noddings (1992) point out that persons can care about a number of things—humans, ideas, things, objects, or causes, to name a few. They further recognize a distinction between caring *about* and caring *for*. In this discussion, I am concentrating on caring that is oriented toward persons and, further, am emphasizing both ethics and activities concerned principally with caring *for*. This is not to say, however, that I am ignoring caring about ideas, causes, or objects. I am simply emphasizing the personal and interpersonal dimensions of this concept and noting other types of care as they contribute to these.

THE PURPOSES OF CARING

Caring does not lend itself readily to an operational definition, for few actions can be labeled universally as caring (Noddings, 1984). However, it can, at least in part, be understood in terms of purposes or goals. In the next section, I discuss two that are basic to any caring endeavor.

Promoting Human Development

In his seminal work, *On Caring* (1971), Milton Mayeroff suggests that caring has as its purpose the fostering of development. Indeed, he argues that the encouragement of personal growth is its defining characteristic. "To care for another person, in the most significant sense, is to help him grow and actualize himself" (p. 1). Asserting that certain common themes can be detected, even though caring may be exhibited in a variety of circumstances, Mayeroff devotes his book to describing and exploring the "general pattern of caring" (p. 1). He argues that caring has its genesis in a special kind of union between persons.

> In caring as helping the other grow, I experience what I care for . . . as an
> extension of myself and at the same time as something separate from me that
> I respect in its own right. (p. 3)

This type of awareness leads to a relationship characterized by hope and faith in the potential of others and, by patience and honesty, in seeking to nurture that potential.

Physician Willard Gaylin (1976) concurs with Mayeroff in regard to the developmental orientation of care. He, too, asserts that caring commitments are teleological in that they presuppose that, in each person, there exist the potential for growth and the propensity to move toward that potential. Seeing similarities between social, emotional, and physical development, Gaylin asserts that tendencies to grow can be nurtured and supported, distorted or misdirected, or, in extreme cases, denied and blocked. For him, true caring occurs when persons relate to others in ways that honor and encourage the healthy unfolding of all types of development.

Both Mayeroff and Gaylin concentrate on caring as an other-directed activity and commitment. They acknowledge, however, that a complete understanding of this idea must include the recognition that care for another and care for self are linked. These authors also agree on what might be called the "natural-ness" of caring. That is, they assert that human beings are ontologically rela-tional and that caring interactions represent the natural and appropriate expres-sion of this reality.

Additional support for these ideas can be found in the writings of Jewish philosopher Martin Buber, protestant theologician/philosopher John Macmur-ray, feminist educator and philosopher Nel Noddings, and psychoanalyst Erich Fromm. Emphasizing the mutuality of caring, each of them argues that the growth and well-being of all participants in loving, supportive interactions should and will be enhanced.

Asserting that persons are ontologically linked to one another, Buber (1958) suggests that one can enjoy the full experience of "being" (p. 11) only by entering fully and directly into caring, respectful relationships. Within these "I–Thou" relationships, persons become able to love and delight in others, themselves, and the experience of living.

> Love is *between I and Thou*. The man who does not know this, with his very being know this, does not know love. . . . Love ranges in its effect throughout the whole world. In the eyes of him who takes his stand in love, and gazes out of it, men are cut free from their entanglement in bustling activity. Good people and evil, wise and foolish, beautiful and ugly, become successively real to him. (p. 15)

Writing from a slightly different theological perspective, John Macmurray (1933, 1957, 1961) agrees with Buber's assertions. In order to understand his perspective on the goals or outcomes of caring, one must first understand cer-tain of Macmurray's presuppositions. Like Buber, he assumes "the inherent so-ciality of human life" (1957, p. 49). Macmurray also suggests that individuals who fail to recognize this fundamental interrelatedness live incomplete, morally and experientially bankrupt lives. He contrasts these with a set of individuals he labels "persons." For Macmurray, the word *person* describes a "self-conscious [fully aware or alive] being." He asserts that personhood is possible only within caring relationships: "The [personal] self only exists in the commu-nion of selves" (1957, p. 99). For Buber and Macmurray, authentic, joyful life is achieved through participation in I–Thou, personal relationships. Indeed, for them caring is so linked to development that speaking of the latter as a goal of the former might suggest an artificial cause and effect type of relationship. For these philosophers, the "goal" and the process by which it is achieved are re-lated reciprocally, not sequentially. Both, however, do write that potential devel-opment becomes actual in caring, supportive interactions. Thus, their work im-plies that, in a teleological sense, development can be described as a goal of caring.

The realization of genuine personhood is also linked to participation in caring relationships by Noddings (1984), who states that "the relational mode seems to be essential to living fully as a person" (p. 35). She describes a caring interaction and shows how it enhances rather than diminishes one's sense of self and security.

> When I care . . . I do not relinquish myself. . . . I allow my motive energy to be shared; put it at the service of others. It is clear that my vulnerability is potentially increased when I care, for I can be hurt through the other as well as through myself. But my strength and hope are also increased, for if I am weakened, the other, which is a part of me, may remain strong and insistent. (p. 33)

Fromm (1956) stresses that love for others is inextricably linked to "care, respect, responsibility, and knowledge" (p. 50) of oneself.

> To love somebody is the actualization and concentration of the power to love . . . [and] love of one person implies love of man as such. . . . From this it follows that my own self must be as much an object of my love as another person. *The affirmation of one's own life, happiness, growth, freedom is rooted in one's capacity to love.* (p. 50)

Indeed Fromm suggests that loving is possible only for those who love and respect themselves. "If an individual is able to love productively, he loves himself too. If he can love *only* others, he cannot love at all" (p. 50).

Responding to Needs

Carol Gilligan, author of *In a Different Voice* (1982), emphasizes that those who care will recognize that they have a "moral imperative . . . a responsibility to discern the 'real and recognizable trouble' of this world" (p. 100) and to act to alleviate suffering caused by that trouble. Challenging traditional ways of understanding moral development (e.g., Kohlberg, 1966, 1969, 1976), she suggests that male theorists have tended to see morality built on an ethic of principled justice as superior to that built on an ethic of care. Gilligan calls on educators and others whose work is primarily relational in nature to recognize and value the ability to see and respond to needs.

The antecedents of caring actions—those that set the stage for both perceiving and responding to needs—are the starting point for Noddings's (1984) discussion of an ethic of care. She expresses agreement with Gilligan (1982) and Mayeroff (1971) and notes that caring actions grow out of what she terms "motivational displacement" (p. 16), defined as a concern for "the welfare, protection or enhancement of the cared for" (p. 23) as well as for oneself. Noddings also stresses that this motivational state must be linked with a commitment to or "engrossment" (p. 16) with the growth of the recipient of care. When motivational displacement and engrossment join, the person giving care will find herself or himself

> stepping out of one's own personal frame of reference into the other's . . . consider[ing] the other's point of view, his objective needs, and what he expects of us. . . . Reasons for acting, thus, have to do with the [other's] wants and desires and with the objective elements of his problematic situation. (p. 24)

Noddings's discussion makes an important point: An ethic of care encourages consideration of both the subjective and objective elements of situations. One guided by it will certainly attend to the affective, short-term, "felt" needs of others, but will not address these in ways that compromise objective, long-term well-being.

Buber (1958, 1965) emphasizes a specific need with which caring is especially concerned—the need for liberation. Conceiving of this as a personal and spiritual phenomenon, he equates personal liberation as the full realization of one's unique identity with "the release of powers" (1965, p. 90) inherent in each person. For Buber, the final outcome of caring relationships is an encounter with the ultimate *Thou* or God. He writes, however, that all relationships worthy of attention mirror and contribute to a person's encounter with the divine. Thus, he sees in all interactions the potential for furthering personal liberation.

Other scholars echo Buber in stressing that oppression and repression create situations of needs that caring must address. Many, however, emphasize the importance of social, cultural, and economic liberation. Theologian Matthew Fox (1990) writes convincingly of the linkages between addressing a host of individual needs and working for social justice. He states, "The contemporary word for [the] relief of pain is justice making" (p. 11). Fox claims that relieving pain and pursuing justice require bold, creative, and compassionate activity in economic and political arenas alongside loving and supportive behaviors in individual interactions.

Several educational scholars—notably critical theorists (e.g., Bates, 1984; Foster, 1986a, 1986b; Giroux, 1988b; Purpel, 1989) and feminist scholars (e.g., Brabeck, 1989; Eugene, 1989; Higgins, 1989; Noddings, 1984, 1988, 1989, 1992; Shakeshaft, 1987)—echo Fox's views and apply them specifically to educational endeavors. Calling for schooling that honors social justice and compassion, Purpel offers a statement that reflects a dominant thrust of the thinking of these groups. He writes:

> If we are to accept our commitments seriously, educators have a special concern for helping us to be liberated *from* the various conditions that oppress

us, particularly those of ignorance and illiteracy. Freire (1970, 1973) has shown us that ignorance and illiteracy are more than embarrassing and troublesome in that they are necessary ingredients of poverty, hunger, misery, and oppression. (p. 124)

For Purpel, the biblical Exodus story becomes a metaphor for caring liberation. He finds in it not only "the story of the trek to the 'land of milk and honey'" (p. 125), but also guidelines for how such a journey is to be undertaken. Arguing that the genuine marriage of compassion and justice requires both escaping from (and, for all practical purposes, destroying) oppressive forces and constructing communities conducive to development, Purpel suggests that education provides a natural arena for "mak[ing] a world" (p. 125) wherein the goals of caring—healthy sound development and met needs—can be pursued and achieved.

THE CONTEXT OF CARING

Caring, as it is understood by all the authors cited in the previous section, depends on a special kind of relationship between persons, one characterized by some measure of commitment. Mayeroff (1971) calls this commitment "devotion" (p. 5) and suggests that it

> is shown by . . . being "there" for the other in a way that is the converse of holding back and ambivalence. Viewed over an extended period, it is shown by . . . consistency, which expresses itself in persistence under unfavorable conditions and in . . . willingness to overcome difficulties. (p. 6)

Noddings (1984), as noted earlier, labels this same phenomenon "engrossment" and discusses it in terms of "displacement of my own reality to the reality of the other" (p. 14). She supports her ideas by citing Kierkegaard, who wrote of seeing "another's reality as possibility for us [so that] we must act to eliminate the intolerable, to reduce the pain, to fill the need, to actualize the dream" (p. 14), and she states that "when I am in this sort of relationship, when the other's reality becomes a real possibility for me, I care" (p. 14). "Interdependence" is the term selected by Gilligan (1982, p. 149) to describe this relational quality. She writes that, when interdependence exists between people, they are motivated "to act responsively toward self and others and thus to sustain connectivity . . . [and an] ethic of care" (p. 149).

Communities as Settings for Caring

Relationships of this sort obviously can and do exist between individuals or within small groups in dyadic or familial patterns. Many scholars argue, though, that they flourish in environments that stress a sense of community. Hobbs and his co-authors (1984) are among those who propose that a community is important to the development of reciprocal caring relationships. "In communities, individuals experience a sense of membership, influence members of the group, have personal needs fulfilled, and share a psychologically and personally satisfying connection with other people" (p. 41).

In their writing, Hobbs and co-authors focus specifically on the need for communities to foster the development of those who, for some reason, are disabled and thus disadvantaged (relative to the "abled") in quests for material, physical, emotional, and intellectual well-being. Brad Mitchell (1990a, 1990b) agrees with the contention that communities are critical for personal development. He, however, expands Hobbs and his co-authors' arguments, suggesting that virtually everyone in modern culture is disabled due to the "rapid and repeated episodes of loss" (p. 22) that have become commonplace in our lives. As examples of these losses, Mitchell refers to illnesses (both physical and mental), disrupted families, poverty, and other situations that threaten personal and societal well-being. In his view, these crises of loss destroy the sense of security fundamental to living happy, full lives. He suggests that security must be restored and that this can be achieved only if persons sense that they are members of a group or community that cares for and about them. Mitchell, thus, challenges educational leaders to create school communities that support "consistent and continuous nurturance of belonging" (p. 39). This task, he argues, is foundational to educational efforts that enhance the quality of individual and corporate life.

In a similar vein, Kirkpatrick (1986) describes true communities as those characterized by "friendship, fellowship, love, and mutuality" (p. 186). Drawing upon insights of Scottish philosopher/theologian John Macmurray (1933, 1950, 1957, 1961), Kirkpatrick offers several important observations about the antecedents and outcomes of caring interactions. He describes such relationships as "heterocentric, concerned for the Other as Other" (p. 186) and clarifies that this concern is motivated by love that has as its purpose simply the joy of involvement with another. "Here we have the germ of community. Love of the other person for his or her own sake is a love which is intensely delightful. It has no purpose beyond itself" (p. 175).

The Building of "Community" as an Ideal of Caring

In regard to the communities created by this love, Kirkpatrick quotes liberally from Macmurray, noting that the ideal community is a universal one "in which all personal relationships [are] positively motivated, all its members [are] free and equal in relation" (Macmurray, 1950, p. 163, cited in Kirkpatrick, 1986, p. 197) and all people "achieve fellowship and communion" (p. 194). Both scholars acknowledge that such a community is, in a literal sense, impossible both because of resistance within the human spirit and because of the sheer logistical impossibility of universal fellowship. They, however, stress that the reality of this universal caring community is less important than the intention to care in a woman's or man's heart. Kirkpatrick again chooses Macmurray's words to elucidate this concept.

> Community is constituted not solely by its degree of achievement but by the intention which sustains it. This means that in any meeting of persons there is the *potential* for friendship. To love others in community is to recognize and explicitly affirm "the intention which constitutes our personal nature. . . . It is to maintain the disposition and the purpose to care for *any* human being with whom we are brought into relations, in whatever fashion circumstances make possible, and simply on the ground of our common humanity." (Macmurray, 1950, p. 85, cited in Kirkpatrick, 1986, p. 195, emphasis in original)

The relationship between concepts of community and fraternity is the focus of McWilliams (1973), who, noting that American culture is deeply dualistic" (p. 98), describes them as America's "ambiguous ideal[s]" (p. 94). On the one hand is a strong commitment to individualism evident in laws and doctrines that embrace "the social contract [and] the superiority of individual decisions" (p. 97). On the other hand are two traditions that, according to McWilliams, oppose this penchant for individual action. He describes the first as "the myth of *gemeinschaft,* the dream of community which . . . has more than once helped support the effort to conquer nature in the hope that . . . it might lead humanity back to 'oneness'" (p. 99). The second, he states, is "the Judeo-Christian idea of fraternity which . . . has recognized that man's quest to transcend nature is critically dependent on society and politics, and on a fraternity which shares alienation from nature and estrangement from God" (p. 99). McWilliams (and other authors cited in this section) suggests that the health of individuals and of our local, national, and global societies depends on recognizing the legitimacy of both traditions and eschewing a dualistic thinking that pits individuals against their communities. Instead, they call for celebrations of interrelatedness and for the creative search for caring, mutually beneficial ways of relating.

THE ACTIVITIES OF CARING

Caring, as noted in the introduction to this section, is not easily defined in unambiguous, quantifiable terms. It can, however, be understood as a process that involves certain general, but definite and identifiable, activities. Scholars who have explored this topic in depth note that caring always involves, to some degree, three activities. They are: (1) receiving the other's perspective; (2) responding appropriately to the awareness that comes from this reception; and (3) remaining committed to others and to the relationship.

Receiving

The first activity, receiving the other's perspective, involves openness and a willingness to accept another's reality uncritically. Gabriel Marcel (cited in Blackham, 1959, p. 80) describes this more in terms of an attitude than an activity, calling it "disposability [disponibilité], the readiness to bestow and spend oneself and make oneself available." In his discussion of love, Fromm (1956) expresses a similar sentiment, noting that "love is not primarily a relationship to a specific person; it is an *attitude* and *orientation of character* which determines the relatedness of a person to the world as a whole, not toward one 'object of love'" (p. 38). This idea is also found in the writings of Macmurray (1950, 1957), who emphasizes that true caring begins with the intention to care. Macmurray (1950, 1957) and Kirkpatrick (1986) both point out that a variety of factors may dictate against caring actions, and they suggest that in these circumstances, the intention or willingness to care is, for the purposes of discussion, the same as active caring.

A number of scholars, while not ignoring the importance of the intention to care, focus on what occurs when one person actually receives another's perspective. Noddings (1984) describes this phase of caring as "regard, desire for the other's well-being" (p. 19). She chooses Buber's words to describe the activity of receiving. "When I receive the other, I am totally with the other. The relation is for the moment, exactly as Buber has described it in *I and Thou*. The other fills the firmament" (p. 32).

Mayeroff (1971) suggests that knowing is another dimension of receiving,

> To care for someone, I must know many things. I must know, for example, who the other is, what his powers and limitations are, what his needs are, and what is conducive to his growth. I must know how to respond to his needs and what my own powers and limitations are. (p. 9)

Fromm (1956) also emphasizes that knowing is foundational to caring. Arguing that love involves respect, he insists that genuine respect is possible only if one knows another. "To respect a person is not possible without knowing him; care and responsibility would be blind if they were not guided by knowledge" (pp. 23–24).

Martin Buber (1965) discusses the type of knowledge that makes caring possible. He notes that one might relate superficially to another by "observing" or "looking on" but states that caring occurs only when one truly "become[s] aware" (p. 9). Suggesting that awareness grows out of deep understanding and that this deep understanding is possible only when one is open to and accepting of another's reality, Buber is quite willing to acknowledge that these ideas are not easily defined in a completely rational way. Using another metaphor, he writes:

> It is a different matter [from observing or looking on] when in a receptive hour of my personal life a man meets me about whom there is something which I cannot grasp in any objective way at all, that "says something" to me. That does not mean, says to me what manner of man this is, what is going on in him, and the like. But it means, says something *to me*, addresses something to me, speaks something that enters my own life. . . . To understand "say" as a metaphor is not to understand. The phrase "that doesn't say a thing to me" is an outworn metaphor, but the saying I am referring to is real speech. In the house of speech are many mansions, and this is one of the inner. (pp. 9–10, emphasis in original)

Novelist Harper Lee (1960) chooses different images to convey the concept of receiving another's perspective. Early in *To Kill a Mockingbird*, attorney Atticus Finch attempts to explain the basis of positive human interactions to his daughter Scout with these words:

> "First of all," he said, "if you can learn a simple trick, Scout, you'll get along a lot better with all kinds of folk. You never really understand a person until you consider things from his point of view . . . until you climb into his skin and walk around in it." (p. 34)

As the story unfolds, Scout has several opportunities to experience this "climb[ing] into [another's] skin." One of the most moving scenes occurs at the end of the novel when Scout, for the first time, sees Boo Radley, a neighbor who heretofore has been a mysterious and frightening character. Boo is standing, half hidden behind a door in the Finch home, after he has saved the lives of Scout and her brother, Jem. Lee's description of Scout's first moments with Boo beautifully portrays Scout's receiving of Boo Radley's perspective and the caring that follows. As the novel ends, Scout is talking with her father about the deeds for which Boo had been falsely blamed.

> "An' they chased him 'n' never could catch him 'cause they didn't know what he looked like, an' Atticus, when they finally saw him, why he hadn't done any of those things. . . . Atticus, he was real nice. . . ."
> His hands were under my chin, pulling up the cover, tucking it around me.
> "Most people are, Scout, when you finally see them." (pp. 283–284)

Responding

Caring, thus, begins with an attitude of openness and receptivity. Most scholars agree, though, that caring also includes some kind of action on behalf of the one cared for. Several (e.g., Buber, 1965; Fromm, 1956; Gilligan, 1982; Noddings, 1984) note that these actions begin with a willingness on the part of one person to assume responsibility for another. They stress that even as words such as "responsibility" and "response" are linked etymologically, so they are linked in the act of caring. In the words of Buber (1965), "Genuine responsiveness exists where there is real responding" (p. 16).

Noddings (1984) distinguishes between two kinds of responsiveness: One she calls "natural," and the other, "ethical" (p. 79). To find an example of the first, she looks to a mother–child relationship. She suggests that a mother's responses to her child are so natural that they are rarely noticed, planned, or analyzed. In Noddings's estimation, these responses are instinctive and easy to carry out. Indeed, not to respond would be difficult in these situations. She contrasts this natural, often subconscious, responsiveness with caring that grows out of a conscious, willful decision to respond to another. This volitional caring she labels "ethical" and suggests that it is related to a sense of obligation, a conscious belief that "'I must do something' in response to the need of the cared-for" (p. 91). Noddings suggests ethical caring actions are somewhat less instinctive than natural ones. These actions are chosen when the one giving care assesses the situation, the needs of the one receiving care, and the "judgments of significant others" (p. 92), and then acts appropriately to alleviate needs. Regardless of whether the caring is natural or ethical or the actions instinctive or planned, Noddings emphasizes that caring must go beyond an attitude and actualize itself in some kind of action.

Gilligan (1982) also stresses that caring involves both assuming responsibility and acting responsively. She speaks of a sense of responsibility as an "ideal" and as a "strength" (p. 149) and notes that it inevitably leads to actions on behalf of the one cared for. Her discussion of the responsiveness of caring focuses on the ways it is concerned with nurturing and lessening or removing another's needs. Gilligan notes that differences in situations make it impossible to label any particular act as universally or absolutely responsive or caring and suggests that, if labeling is needed, criteria for judgment must be developed for each situation.

Similarly, Buber (1958, 1965) avoids labeling any specific action as caring or responsive. He, however, does offer a kind of standard against which interactions can be evaluated, when he stresses that truly caring actions will be actions that move people toward community. His logic begins with the belief that a state of interrelatedness among people is natural and desirable. In *I and Thou* (1958), he writes, "All real living is meeting" (p. 11), and in *Between Man and*

Man (1965), that "living in real togetherness [and] being able to have confidence within this community compensates for cosmic insecurity" (p. 196). He further notes that people suffer in the absence of this "connexion and certainty" (p. 196).

> If the organic community disintegrates from within . . . mistrust becomes life's basic note. . . . The unaffectedness of wishing is stifled by mistrust, everything around is hostile or can become hostile, agreement between one's own and the other's desire ceases, for there is not true coalescence or reconciliation with what is necessary to sustain community, and the dulled wishes creep helplessly into the recesses of the soul. (p. 197)

Buber's ideas support a notion discussed earlier: Caring actions will move toward the development or support of genuine communities.

Fromm (1956) divides his discussion of loving actions according to their objects. He deals with brotherly love, the love of a parent for a child, erotic love, self-love, and love of God, and notes that actions within these diverse categories have four characteristics in common: "care, responsibility, respect, and knowledge" (p. 22). By equating care with "an active concern for the life and growth of that which we love," Fromm suggests that caring actions will always be in the direction of the growth and development of another. In regard to responsibility, he writes, "To be 'responsible' means to be able and ready to 'respond'" (p. 23). These words suggest an element of caring actions that has not heretofore been discussed. That is, they require not only an attitude of willingness, but also conscious preparation on the part of the one offering care. The idea that caring requires effort is implicit also in Fromm's words on the concept of respect. Reminding readers that relationships are not always convenient, he states that true love deals with the other *"as he is,* not as I need for him to be" (p. 24, emphasis in the original). In his discussion of this dimension of love, Fromm emphasizes that one can offer respect only if she or he possesses inner strength and courage, if one "can stand and walk without crutches" (p. 24). Finally, he notes that care, responsibility, and respect must be based in a knowledge "which penetrates to the core" (p. 24) of others and their situations. In saying this, he clearly links the responses of love to the receiving of another's reality, the first phase of caring discussed in this section. Fromm stresses that this deep, inner knowledge of another is possible only if a person "transcend[s] the prison of separateness" (p. 24) and allows another to enter her or his life, mind, and heart.

The discussion of caring responses, thus far, has focused on the attitudes and the actions of the person giving care. A more complete understanding must also take into account the experiences of the one receiving care. Indeed, Buber (1958, 1965), Mayeroff (1971), and Kelsey (1981) note that caring is fundamentally a reciprocal interaction and that the responses of the recipient are as pivotal to the process as the actions of the giver.

The metaphor of a dialogue is used by Buber (1958, 1965) to picture the reciprocal nature of caring. With this image, he richly conveys the idea that interactions between persons are never unilateral. He notes that a person who receives care may play a fairly inactive role in some interactions (e.g., young pupil with teacher or infant child with parent) but stresses that even these involve a continuing process of "giving and taking" (1965, p. 100). In relationships between equals (e.g., friends or lovers), he labels interaction as dialogical and "mutual" (p. 101). Regardless of the degree of mutuality, Buber stresses that the perspectives of all involved parties must be considered to determine if true caring responses have been offered and received. If this occurs, both parties will experience and reflect "trust, trust in the world because [the other] human being exists" (p. 98).

In a similar vein, Mayeroff (1971) suggests that each party in a caring relationship will have certain emotional responses because of the other's action. He first takes the perspective of the person receiving care to describe this individual's affective response.

> When the other is with me, I feel I am not alone. I feel understood not in some detached way but because I feel he knows what it is like to be me. I realize that he wants to see me as I am, not in order to pass judgment on me, but to help me. I do not have to conceal myself by trying to appear better than I am; instead I can open myself up for him, let him get close to me. (p. 31)

Mayeroff then turns his attention to the emotions of the one who gives and states that this person frequently experiences "spontaneous delight or joy" because of the growth and development of the cared for.

Kelsey (1981), in turn, emphasizes that caring happens only if the one cared for knows that she or he has been nurtured or loved. "Love is an experiential reality. . . . We have either known what it is to be loved and to love, or we know little or nothing" (p. 8). Furthermore, he declares, "My love is never complete until the other person feels more loved by me. . . . [Love] continues to love other human beings until they feel loved. [When this happens] I am not loving merely when I feel loving, but when others feel loved and cared for by me" (p. 15).

Remaining

Kelsey's emphasis on love's continuance points to the final phase of caring, a phase I have labeled "remaining." By this, I do not imply that the constant, never ending, literal presence of people in relationships is, in most cases, either necessary or desirable. I do suggest, though, that caring involves commitment, a commitment that is stronger than the desire to run. Mayeroff calls this commitment "devotion" and proposes that it "develops in the process of overcoming obstacles and difficulties" (p. 5).

Noddings (1984) clarifies that this devotion means not constant attention, but constant willingness to give attention if the situation demands it. Buber (1958) expresses the same idea when he writes that love "endures . . . in the alteration of actuality and latency" (p. 69), and Richard Niebuhr (1956), who forthrightly declares "love is loyalty" (p. 35), stresses that in caring one will be continually aware of and responsive to, but not necessarily physically present with, the one who is loved. Similar ideas can also be found in Fromm's (1956) discussion of the constancy of love or caring. He notes that as relationships change over time, the form that caring takes changes, but the fact of caring or loving as an attitude does not. He offers a parent's relationship with her or his child as an example, noting that actions change in this type of relationship, but that caring, if it is real at all, remains even when circumstances change.

For Gilligan (1982), remaining as a part of caring is a correlate of acting responsibly. One of the young women she interviewed in a study reported in *In a Different Voice* defined the word *responsibility* in the following way: "[It means] that other people are counting on you to do something and you can't just decide, 'Well, I'd rather do this or that'" (p. 37). Gilligan concurs with this definition and suggests that such an attitude is critical to caring and that it indicates a high level of moral development. Similarly, Bellah and his colleagues (1985) suggest that members of caring communities will embrace long-term responsibility not only for themselves, but also for others. Choosing the word *commitment* (p. 160) to describe the intention to continue in caring interactions regardless of transient feelings, they contrast "long-term commitments . . . [with] desires and feelings" (p. 161). These authors note that a sense of "solidarity" (p. 162) among community members seems to encourage such commitments.

Two others who speak of the ongoing willingness to care as commitment are anthropologist Margaret Mead (1970) and psychiatrist Kenneth Keniston (1965). Mead suggests that commitment to others in interdependent relationships grows out of a sense of "living connection" (p. 79) and that such commitment is necessary if members of modern cultures are to live healthy and satisfying lives. Keniston's (1965) understanding of this attitude can be derived from his descriptions of lives that evidence no sense of connection. He relates a lack of commitment to "alienation, estrangement, disaffection, anomie, withdrawal, disengagement, separation, non-involvement, apathy, indifference, and neutralism—all . . . point[ing] to a sense of loss, a growing gap between men and their social world" (p. 3). Furthermore, he writes that "the drift of our time is away from connection, relation, communion, and dialogue" (p. 3). Clearly, he views commitment as an attitude that promotes a sense of caring, ongoing involvement with others.

One of the facets of care that must be considered, if one accepts the fact that it entails responsibility and constancy or remaining, is that it will, at some point in time, require sacrifice. Interestingly, those who write about this are virtually unanimous in their assertion that this sacrifice enhances, rather than diminishes, the experience of the one making it. For Buber (1958, 1965), Fromm (1956), Noddings (1984), and Niebuhr (1956), this enhancement occurs because of the union of the caring and the cared for. Buber (1958) emphasizes this union by linking the words *I* and *Thou,* calling them together "one primary word" (p. 3). Niebuhr (1956) equates being bound to another in love with "rejoicing," "happiness," and "satisfaction" (p. 35), and suggests that the power of these feelings overwhelms any sense of loss when love's continuance requires sacrifice. In turn, Noddings believes that a frequent outcome that accompanies the embracing of another's needs is something she calls "joy" (p. 132). She writes that "joy often accompanies a realization of our relatedness. It is the special affect that arises out of the receptivity of caring, and it represents a major reward for the one caring" (p. 132).

Fromm (1956) suggests that caring's sacrifice as a negative experience is valid only in a capitalistic, individualistic culture where individual achievement and acquisition are viewed as principal goals of human interaction, and actions that might lessen the attainment of these goals are viewed as undesirable. Gilligan (1982) and Noddings (1984), with a similar line of reasoning, indict not capitalism, but paternalism as misunderstanding sacrifice and caring. They claim that male dominated views of life, ethics, and power have led our culture to value actions that lead to accomplishment and to devalue actions that nurture another if they involve some kind of personal sacrifice.

An excellent example of caring's constancy, even when sacrifice is required, can be found in Mark Twain's classic novel, *The Adventures of Huckleberry Finn* (1981, originally published in 1885). In this tale, Huck Finn learns to see his companion and runaway slave, Jim, as a person with human needs and feelings, and he learns to care for Jim even as Jim cares for him. At one point in the story, Huck contemplates turning Jim over to the authorities. His culture has taught him that this would be morally right. Indeed, Huck has been led to believe that he risks punishment in hell if he does not turn in Jim. In a moving passage of the novel, Huck grapples with his culture and his conscience and finally decides, "All right, then, I'll go to hell" (p. 206), rather than betray his friend. In doing this he vividly demonstrates that caring compels the one offering it to remain with the cared for even if it involves sacrifice or loss. Significantly, in Twain's story the decision to remain faithful to Jim brings Huck peace and satisfaction, and he learns that the rewards of caring outweigh any price that the giver of care might have to pay.

SUMMARY

Caring, as both ethic and action, has certain features that distinguish it. It is a basic human activity that has as a goal the well-being of another, well-being that might be understood variously as growth and development, as met needs and satisfied desires, or as political or spiritual liberation. Caring proceeds in the context of interdependent relationships in networks that might be labeled communities. The communal relationships between people mean that the welfare of each is inextricably related to the welfare of others so that one caring for others in fact cares for herself or himself.

Connections between people in communities facilitate the process of caring, a process that begins with the act of receiving others' perspectives of reality. When one opens to receive another, she or he begins to assume responsibility for the other's welfare. This responsibility is actualized when one responds, in some way, to another person. This responding can take almost any form, depending on the situation. It will, however, always seek to be consistent with the goals of caring. It will also, in some way, involve reciprocal transactions wherein the one caring and the one cared for give to each other.

Caring is, finally, distinguished by the fact that there is commitment between the people who care. This commitment shifts caring from being a conditional act dependent on merit or whim, and moves it toward being an unconditional act marked by acceptance, nurturance, and grace. This unconditional nature of caring is, obviously, an ideal. However, it is a reality to the extent that people, living with an awareness of their interdependence, strive to cultivate and maintain a sense of community and to act in ways that further the welfare and growth and development both of others and of themselves.

2 Justifications for a Caring Ethic: Deontological Arguments

> I am thrilled by the beauty and rationality of the universe, from quarks to the human brain, its order, intricacy and integration. Personal relationships are a part of that order. They are a clue to the nature of ultimate reality. The personal is the highest category we know, and it can't be reduced to atoms and molecules. It is a reality in its own right.
>
> (Dr. Arthur Peacocke, Molecular Biologist and Dean of Clare College, Oxford, England, December 1990, p. 71)

In *After Virtue: A Study in Moral Theory* (1981), Alisdair MacIntyre discusses the "interminable character" (p. 6) of moral debates. He notes that arguments advocating different, even opposite, positions, can all be "logically valid or can easily be expanded so as to be made so" (p. 8). This fact, however, in MacIntyre's view, does not mean that ethical discussion must necessarily be irrational. Indeed, he notes that the fact that various moral positions use logic to defend their "particular arguments . . . presuppose[s] a systematic, although often unstated account of rationality" (p. 242). Jeffrey Stout (1988), in a similar vein, notes that "disagreement and diversity in ethics" (p. 13) and the reality that divergent views can be rationally justified do not demand that scholars must "abandon the traditional conception of moral judgment and reasoning" (p. 13). He states that his purpose in *Ethics After Babel* is to "try to show simply that the facts of moral diversity don't compel us to become nihilists or skeptics" (p. 14). One premise central to his argument is that moral truths do exist and that lack of knowledge, disbelief, or disregard of these truths does not destroy their existence or importance.

Following Stout (1988) and numerous other scholars, I propose the existence of certain ethical verities. With him, I acknowledge that

> some of the moral propositions that [I] embrace, however justified [I] may be in accepting them under current epistemic circumstances will someday be discovered to be false. That is, they are false now, even though [I] don't know it yet, even though [I'm] now justified in accepting them as true. (p. 25)

21

The awareness that my knowledge is incomplete certainly humbles me as I argue that caring is a right and useful ethic for educational administrators. It does not, however, deter me in attempting to build a logical conceptual framework for understanding the place of this ethic in the practice and study of school leadership. The words of Stout (1988) and models suggested by Frankena (1973) and Strike, Haller, and Soltis (1988) were especially useful as I organized and wrote the next two chapters.

Stout (1988) makes a critical distinction between the concepts of "justification and truth" (p. 25). He notes that justification of a particular view of truth is an activity demanding clarity of thought and logical reasoning. According to Stout, justification cannot *prove* truth. It can, however, present compelling evidence in support of a particular view. Frankena (1973) suggests that justifications of ethical positions can be broadly classified as either deontological or teleological. The former are arguments that look to the fundamental nature of an act or principle to assess morality or immorality. Teleological justifications, in Frankena's schema, in contrast, look to results to judge morality and assume that moral acts are those which "produce a greater balance of good over evil than any available alternative" (p. 14). Using a similar classification system, Strike and co-authors (1988) write of nonconsequentialist and consequentialist ethical theories. The former look to a premise for guidance, while the latter "rely solely on consequences to judge the morality of an action" (p. 19).

I divide my discussions of justifications for an ethic of caring according to whether they stress deontological or consequentialist rationales. This classification system has two strengths to recommend it. First, it provides an organized system for discussing diverse arguments. Second, it offers a framework from which I can address concerns of persons holding a range of ideas about the purposes of education and the role of administrators. However, the artificial nature of this classification system runs the risk of drawing distinctions that, in fact, do not exist. Many of the arguments, for example, that I label as deontological have teleological or consequentialist elements, for inherent in them is the assumption that actions, intrinsically right, will result in the greatest balance of good over evil. I attempt to address this weakness by focusing, in this chapter, on arguments that stress that principles derived from the fundamental nature of reality provide justification for a caring ethic. I begin with points made by those who claim that a caring deity has created persons in such a way that their humanity is most fully realized in caring interactions. These are followed by arguments offered by scholars who believe that giving and receiving care are intrinsically human characteristics. Some of those cited believe that these characteristics have a divine origin; others do not. What they share is an emphasis on the fact that the need and desire to participate in nurturing interactions are basic and natural to persons. The third set of arguments discussed in this chapter comes from those who emphasize that history and tradition tell of an ongoing quest, on a societal and organizational level, for a sense of community. They emphasize that a caring ethic is appropriate in educational institutions because it is consistent with the nature not only of individuals, but also of the social networks they inhibit.

ARGUMENTS BASED ON CONCEPTIONS OF GOD OR OF TRANSCENDENT REALITY

At the heart of these arguments are three assumptions. The first is that a supreme being exists; the second, that this being cares for people; and the third, that this deity intends or desires that people care. These assumptions, if accepted, have relevance for all social structures, including schools and school systems. In this section, I begin by examining the work of scholars who explore some general implications of a belief in a caring deity, and conclude by reviewing the work of some who have applied these ideas specifically to education and educational leadership. I acknowledge that many great thinkers do not accept the central assumptions of this argument, and, in later sections, offer other ideas about the need for a caring ethic in human transactions that do not depend on a belief in a supreme being. I begin with these, though, because the concept that a Creator God exists and cares and that people, created in the image of this God, should both give and receive care, is, for those who accept it, a compelling and logical argument for embracing this ethic.

Caring as an Extension of Belief in a Caring Deity

The words of John Macmurray (1961) articulately express these assumptions and underscore the links between belief in a caring God, an ethic of care, and a commitment to community.

> The essential condition for realizing the universal community is that the world be conceived as the act of God, the creator of the world, and ourselves as created agents, with a limited and dependent freedom to determine the future, which can be realized only on the condition that our intentions are in harmony with His intention, and which must frustrate itself if they are not. (p. 222)

Concurring with this statement, Kirkpatrick asserts:

> According to the biblical tradition, the love which binds God's human creation together with him and with itself is the love known as agape, the community-creating force which God has released into the world and by which his intention for community will be realized. Community is the work

of both God and human persons but its realization or achievement is sustained by the very condition of reality itself because they are themselves God's creation and thus support God's intention. As Martin Luther King, Jr. put it, "All human efforts to establish community are supported by the laws of the universe because God created the universe that way." (Smith & Zepp, 1974, p. 131, cited in Kirkpatrick, 1986, p. 139)

Martin Buber is another proponent of this proposition. In *I and Thou* (1958), he argues that a relationship with a supreme being—referred to by Buber as "the eternal *Thou*" (p. 100) and "the absolute person" (p. 136)—provides a foundation and model for other relationships. Embedded in his views is the belief that this being possesses—indeed, is characterized by—a relational nature. The existence of such a deity constitutes, for Buber, an ethical imperative.

> As a Person, God gives personal life, he makes us as persons become capable of meeting with him and with one another. . . . We can dedicate to him not merely our persons but also our relations to one another. The man who turns to him therefore need not turn away from any other I-Thou relation; but he properly brings them to him, and lets them be fulfilled "in the face of God." (p. 136)

Poet and playwright T. S. Eliot also believed that caring relationships are possible only when people acknowledge the reality of a caring God. In Eliot's early work, prior to his conversion to Christianity, he vividly portrays a world in which people are isolated from one another, uncaring and unfeeling. After Eliot's acceptance of Christianity, his images change drastically. People are no longer portrayed as "hollow men" ("The Hollow Men," 1925, p. 56, in Eliot, *The Complete Poems and Plays*, 1971°) doomed to lonely, fearful lives. In his view, caring, commitment, and love are possible because of God's redemptive acts toward women and men. Eliot describes the life of one who is caring as demonstrating "ardour and selflessness and self-surrender" ("The Dry Salvages," 1941, p. 136) and notes that such a life is possible because of God's love, manifested, in his view, in the incarnation of Christ. In "Choruses from the Rock" (1934), he indirectly answers the question: "How can we love our neighbour?" with these words:

> You have built well, have you forgotten the cornerstone? Talking of right relations of men, but not, of relations of men to GOD.

°All references from T. S. Eliot are taken from Eliot, T. S. (1971). *The complete poems and plays, 1909–1950.* New York: Harcourt, Brace, & World, and page numbers refer to this volume. In the text the original dates are given to place the references in chronological perspective.

"Our citizenship is in Heaven"; yes, but that is the model and type for your citizenship upon earth. (1934/1971, p. 100)

Catholic theologian Jacques Maritain also links faith in the existence of a caring God with a person's willingness and ability to care for another. Throughout *The Person and the Common Good* (1947), he explores the questions: Does loving God first and foremost mean that we must be less responsive to the needs of humans? and, conversely, Does intensely loving humans mean that we might be less concerned with a relationship to God? Maritain argues that love for God should be a moral priority, but that this love will enhance, not hinder, a person's ability and desire to care for other people. Indeed, he suggests that one can truly love others only when she or he first loves God. Maritain finds support for his contention that love for God and love for people are linked from St. Augustine and from St. Thomas Aquinas. The former writes of an ideal society, at least partially realizable, in this life where "the perfectly ordered and harmonious enjoyment of God" coexists with the enjoyment of "one another in God." Aquinas, in turn, asserts that friendship with others is a "concomitant" of one's relationship with God (cited in Maritain, 1947, p. 23).

Still another scholar arguing that the ethic of caring finds its impetus in the caring actions of God is French sociologist Jacques Ellul. In *Jesus and Marx: From Gospel to Ideology* (1988), he examines the implications of various interpretations of Christian thought as they relate to political movements and to human transactions. He concludes that the teachings of the Old and New Testament provide guidelines that, if followed, will result in the "transformation of humanity" (p. 176), something, according to Ellul, sought but not achieved by numerous sociopolitical movements. With a striking choice of words, he labels the Christian ideology that supports human transformation as "anarchist" (p. 174), a term he associates with opposition to political power. Ellul stresses that true anarchy, if it is conceived of in this way, can never use power to oppose power. Rather, he suggests that true "Christian anarchy" will operate from a base of love and will result in "the transformation of humanity . . . [wherein] people become capable of living with others, serving them, as an expression of freedom" (p. 175).

Educational Implications of Belief in a Caring Deity

Those who hold ethical systems derived from beliefs about the nature, desires, and commands of God see all human interactions as coming under some basic imperatives. Some especially emphasize that educational enterprises must be guided by moral impulses that originate with God. Buber is one who explicitly states that education must operate under ethics that support relationships among people and between people and God. In "Education" (1965) he writes that the only moral relationship between the educator and the educated "is one of pure dialogue" (p. 98), a phrase that for Buber conveys a deep sense of responsiveness and caring. He notes that the need for this responsive dialogue in education grows out of two related realities. One is that God, "the great Love" (p. 98), exists as the originator of all "constructive forces" (p. 101) that bind people to one another and to God. The second is that each human being is created in the image of this God. If education is to help people develop their creative and intellectual powers, it must, according to Buber, recognize its purpose as forming "the image of God" (p. 102) within those who are being educated and empowered. He concludes his discussion of education by describing what he believes to be the calling of the educator. It is to "expose himself and others to the creative Spirit [and to] call upon the Creator to save and perfect His image" (p. 103).

In *The Abolition of Man: How Education Develops Man's Sense of Morality* (1947), C. S. Lewis, Fellow and Tutor of English Literature at Magdalen College in Oxford, England, literary critic, author, and Christian apologist, offers an articulate and compelling discussion of the ways in which religion's acceptance of certain truths that transcend reason can and should affect education. He argues that educational attempts to "debunk" (p. 41) religious beliefs and to teach only what is "'rational,' 'biological,' or 'modern'" (p. 33) result in the dehumanization of persons and the destruction of the society in which they live. Using a vivid image, he writes that an education that focuses exclusively on the intellect and denies the heart leads to what may be called "Men without Chests" (p. 34). For Lewis, the chest, or the heart, is associated with the ability to respond emotionally to the world, to God, and to others, and, for him, any educational effort that ignores the "chest," focusing only on the head, is futile, ludicrous, and ultimately destructive.

> We continue to clamour for those very qualities [to be produced by education] we are rendering impossible. . . . In a sort of ghastly simplicity we remove the organ and demand the function. We make men without chests and expect of them virtue and enterprise. We laugh at honour and are shocked to find traitors in our midsts. We castrate and bid the geldings be fruitful. . . . The practical result of [this kind of education] must be the destruction of the society which accepts it. (pp. 35, 39)

It is noteworthy that Lewis, himself a Christian, does not feel that only the Christian religion offers the kind of grounding in absolutes that makes education effective. He indicates that any teaching that acknowledges the possibility of metaphysical truth, "Platonic, Aristotelian, Stoic, Christian, and Oriental alike" (p. 28), can provide a base for effective education.

Using a vision metaphor, Parker Palmer (1983) writes of ways spiritual realities can and should affect educational practices.

Many of us live one-eyed lives. We rely largely on the eye of the mind to form our image of reality. But today more and more of us are opening the other eye, the eye of the heart, looking for realities to which the mind's eye is blind. Either eye alone is not enough. We need "wholesight," a vision of the world in which mind and heart unite "as my two eyes make one in sight." Our seeing shapes our being. Only as we see whole can we and our world be whole.

With the mind's eye we see a world of fact and reason. It is a cold and mechanical place, but we have built our lives there because it seemed predictable and safe. Today, in the age of nuclear science, our mind-made world has been found flawed and dangerous, even lethal. So we open the eye of the heart and see another sight: a world warmed and transformed by the power of love, a vision of community beyond the mind's capacity to see. We cannot forsake our hearts and yet we cannot abandon our minds. How shall we bring together these two lines of sight? (p. xi)

Palmer suggests that an answer to this question can be found, at least in part, by looking to "spiritual tradition" (p. xii).

For Palmer, a delving into the spiritual bases of education will result in a radical reconceptualization of the origins and purposes of schooling. Noting that traditional views hold that the search for knowledge within education usually grows either out of "curiosity or [a desire to] control" (p. 8), he suggests that

. . . another kind of knowledge is available to us. . . . This is a knowledge that originates not in curiosity or control but in compassion, or love—a source celebrated not in our intellectual tradition but in our spiritual heritage. (p. 8)

Palmer devotes much of his work to discussing specific ways educators can discover and implement "models and methods of knowing as an act of love" (p. 9), tasks that for him occur within "a community of faithful relationships" (p. 42). His primary focus is on the teacher's role in bringing about such a community, but his discussion also applies to the work of administrators.

The premises of Buber (1965), Lewis (1947), Palmer (1983), and others cited in this section have clear implications for educational leaders. First, administrators who believe that a caring God desires or commands an ethic of care to govern human interactions will seek to respond to those with whom they work as people rather than as objects. In Buber's words, they will recognize teachers, students, parents, and other administrators as "Thou's" rather than as "It's." They will seek to understand the perspectives of those with whom they work and to consider those perspectives as their own when making decisions. They will recognize and delight in the interdependence of all within their school or school system, and they will continually search for concrete ways to encourage caring relationships between those whom they lead.

ARGUMENTS BASED ON CONCEPTIONS OF PERSONS
OR OF IMMANENT REALITY

A second nonconsequentialist or deontological category of arguments for the ethic of caring in educational administration finds its basis in the belief that participation in caring interactions is central to being fully and completely human. Some who hold this perspective stress that people are, by nature, social, gravitating toward relationships appropriately governed by an ethic of care (e.g., Bellah et al., 1985; Buber, 1958, 1965; Fromm, 1956; Hobbs et al., 1984; McWilliams, 1973; Noddings, 1984). Others, although agreeing with this basic premise, emphasize the "naturalness" and psychological legitimacy of seeking ways to give care (e.g., Gilligan, 1982; Noddings, 1984). Still others focus on the human need to receive care (e.g., Brofenbrenner, 1978; Mitchell, 1990a, 1990b; Noddings, 1984). In this section I review the work of scholars who write from the perspective that caring is an activity consistent with human nature. I basically organize my discussion according to the three premises just noted. That is, I first look at the work of those who argue that interrelatedness is a natural human state and that ethics that promote healthy expressions of this interrelatedness are desirable because of their congruence with nature. I then review the writing of scholars who look at this issue from the perspective of those giving care, arguing that seeking to nurture others is an instinctive human activity. Finally, I examine the work of those who focus on the natural need of persons to receive care. The arguments offered in this section differ slightly from those discussed in the preceding section in that they include some that have been derived from empirical studies on motivation and moral reasoning, as well as philosophical or theoretical arguments on the naturalness of caring.

As in the previous section, the focus shifts from discussions of the basic place of caring in general human transactions to an exploration of its inherent appropriateness for educators. Indeed, several scholars propose that the goals of caring and the basic goals of education are, by their very nature, so similar that a caring ethic is or should be a fundamental component of the world views of administrators and teachers. In some instances, the arguments offered for the basic place of such an ethic in education overlap with those discussed in the closing section of this chapter, which explore historical and traditional evidence that caring, nurturing, community-building perspectives and actions are appropriate within school systems. To some extent, such an overlap is inevitable, for, as noted earlier, moral reasoning does not lend itself to neat classification schemes. I do, however, attempt to make something of a distinction between rationales that rest on an understanding of the basic nature of persons and those that look to history or tradition for justification of a caring ethic. Two guidelines influenced my thinking. In this section, I emphasize arguments that propose that it is the nature of individual persons and, logically by extension, individual administrators to seek to give and receive nurturance. In the following section, I explore works that suggest that schools as organizations are, by their very nature, especially suited for caring interactions.

Caring as an Intrinsically Human Activity

Erich Fromm (1956) is among those who view the desire and capacity for love as factors distinguishing persons from nonhuman forms of life. Arguing that "any theory of love must begin with a theory of man, of human existence" (p. 6), Fromm begins his theory of human existence by proposing that "the deepest need of man . . . is the need to overcome his separateness, to leave the prison of his aloneness" (p. 8). He believes that caring, loving relationships offer the only valid escape from a state of separatedness. Fromm's work is not merely an inspirational treatise on love. It is, rather, an address to academicians, politicians, educators, and others, calling for the study of this "interpersonal union," with consideration of difficulties involved in the loving practices and the discovery of ways to overcome these difficulties and to encourage caring interactions. His justification for devoting a scholarly work to what many might consider a sentimental topic, again, relates to his view that loving is central to human development.

Buber (1965) also writes of the natural desire for mutually caring relationships within some kind of kinship network. In fact, for Buber, this desire for relationships is the distinguishing mark of humanity. He stresses that anyone wishing to gain a deep understanding of persons must consider not only individuals, but relationships.

> The essence of man which is special to him can be directly known only in a living relationship. . . . I and Thou exist only in our world, because man exists, and the I, moreover, exists only through the relation to the Thou. The philosophical science of man, which includes anthropology and sociology, must take as its starting-point the consideration of this subject, "man with man." If you consider the individual by himself, then you see of man just as much as you see of the moon; only man with man provides a full image. If you consider the aggregate by itself, then you see of man just as much as we see of the Milky Way; only man with man is a completely outlined form. Consider man with man, and you see human life, dynamic, twofold, the giver and the receiver, he who does and he who endures, the attacking force and the defending force, the nature which investigates and the nature which supplies information, the request begged and granted—and always both together, completing one another in mutual contribution. (p. 205)

Buber recognizes that forces within life and society strive against I–Thou relationships. It is, however, his contention that social structures that result from anything other than mutually caring, dialogical interactions between persons lead to "an organized atrophy of human existence" (p. 31).

Buber (1958, 1965) roots his arguments that caring is a natural human activity in a belief that a caring God created persons to care. The writing of Noddings (1984) offers an interesting contrast to the work of those who believe an ethic of care is based on "Divine Command" (Frankena, 1973, p. 28) in that she believes that a caring ethic need not find its justification in divine mandates. For Noddings, the observable reality that people gravitate toward relationships, relationships that, on some level, call for interdependence and, perhaps, compassion, leads her to describe "relation as ontologically basis [which] simply means that . . . human encounter and affective response [are] basic fact[s] of human existence" (p. 4). She rejects the idea that a belief in God is a necessary foundation for a caring ethic, arguing that "human love, human caring [is] quite enough on which to found an ethic" (p. 29).

The Naturalness of Giving Care

Several scholars who agree that caring is a basic human activity emphasize especially the naturalness and appropriateness of giving care. Many, like Noddings, are feminists who are calling for a reconsideration of the value of activities that have as their goal the nurturing of another person. Perhaps the seminal work voicing this perspective is Gilligan's *In a Different Voice* (1982). Building a theoretical framework out of several empirical studies on male and female moral reasoning, Gilligan argues that theories that downgrade the values of caring and nurturing reveal "a limitation in the conception of human condition, an omission of certain truths about life" (p. 20). She ultimately calls for the recognition of the moral and psychological legitimacy of an "ethic of responsibility [that] rests on an understanding that gives rise to compassion and care" (p. 165). Significantly, she notes that this ethic of responsibility is typically, but not exclusively, feminine. Her perspective is that the recognition of this ethic by both men and women will lead to "a changed understanding of human development and a more generative view of human life" (p. 174).

Noddings (1984), like Gilligan, contends that offering care is natural because relatedness, "that which connects [one person] naturally to others" (p. 49), is fundamental to the human experience. In her discussion of care giving, Noddings articulately describes several aspects of this phenomenon, including empathy, guilt, the relationship between thinking and feeling, and the differences in asymmetrical and reciprocal relationships. She discusses empathy as a "feeling with" (p. 30) another and notes that often this occurs in a completely natural way (as mothers who "naturally feel with their infants" [p. 31]). In other situations, where empathy is less of a given, she writes that it occurs when persons are in a "receptive state" (p. 30), with "manipulative efforts . . . at rest" (p.

30). In all of these situations, Noddings describes becoming aware of others' needs as an "occurrence," something that naturally happens under given conditions.

The Natural Need to Receive Care

Noddings also devotes a portion of her book to exploring the need for care, a need she believes exists in all persons and especially in children. She suggests that every person has basic needs for acceptance and for recognition of her or his personhood, and she proposes that children must experience the alleviation of these needs if they are to successfully complete all the developmental tasks they face. Quoting Brofenbrenner (1978), she writes:

> The . . . nature of caring is recognized, by, for example, Urie Brofenbrenner when he claims: "In order to develop, a child needs the enduring, irrational involvement of one or more adults in care and joint activity with the child." In answer to what he means by "irrational," he explains, "Somebody has got to be crazy about that kid!" (p. 61).

She also notes that "Brofenbrenner suggests . . . that children embraced in such . . . relationships gain competence; that is, they become able to master situations of greater and greater complexity through their cooperation with adults" (p. 62). Certainly these ideas have a consequential focus in that they point to positive outcomes of caring relationships. They are, however, also nonconsequential in that Noddings and Brofenbrenner both suggest that the results of such interactions are positive because they are consistent with basic needs and inclinations of persons.

Using slightly different terminology, Mitchell (1990a, 1990b) offers similar views. Arguing that all people, but especially children, need to receive care in order to develop into competent, emotionally healthy persons, Mitchell speaks of caring as an activity that nurtures a sense of belonging. Claiming that "human development rests upon three rather simple themes—loss, belonging, and becoming" (1990a, p. 21), Mitchell discusses "belonging" as a state that necessarily precedes "becoming." As noted earlier, he emphasizes that the last decades of the twentieth century have been ones of great and serious loss for both children and adults. Having made this point, Mitchell calls for caring, nurturing relationships to respond to this loss, for he believes such relationships encourage a sense of belonging and that this ultimately also facilitates the process of becoming (or development). These arguments reflect a blend of deontological and consequentialist reasoning. They are discussed in this section, however, because Mitchell depicts "belonging" and "becoming" as natural phenomena. Furthermore, he proposes that the positive outcomes of these process-outcomes that include "strong, happy, and confident children" (1990a, p. 38), "child and family well-being" (1990a, p. 42), and the encouragement of "individual creativity/autonomy and collective effectiveness/accountability" (1990b, p. 68)—are good, at least in part, because they reflect the unfolding of natural processes.

Educational Implications of the Belief That Caring Is a Human Phenomenon

Noddings (1984, 1988, 1992) and Mitchell (1990a, 1990b) both address many remarks directly to educators, emphasizing the importance of acting in nurturing ways that promote a sense of security and belonging in students. In *Caring* (1984), Noddings notes two distinct responsibilities in this regard. First, she calls on educational leaders "to provide an environment in which affection and support are enhanced, in which children not passionately loved will at least receive attention and, perhaps, learn to respond and encourage those who genuinely address them" (p. 61). Second, she challenges educators to search for ways to foster caring attitudes in children so that each child "may . . . someday be 'crazy about' some other child" (p. 61). In this book and in later works (1988, 1992), Noddings offers specific suggestions regarding ways an ethic of care might affect educational practices. She notes, for example, that administrators, parents, policy makers, and others must reevaluate the qualities desired in educators, and she advocates prizing kindness, compassion, and the commitment to seek the well-being of others (1984). Noddings (1988, 1992) also recommends curricular and structural changes for schools. For instance, she suggests that children, especially in the primary grades, stay with one teacher for several years. This, she asserts, would offer greater opportunities for the building of close, caring relationships between students and the adult they see on a daily basis. Additionally, she proposes a reconceptualization of appropriate, moral curriculum. For Noddings, two issues should figure prominently in planning in this area. Schools should teach students how to accept care and, later, to give it and should provide "a curriculum tailored to their individual capacities and interests, one that will provide assurances that there are many acceptable and satisfying ways of life" (1992, p. 30).

Mitchell (1990a) challenges "educational leaders [to] take a hard look at which norms of belonging dominate the public school experience of most students" (p. 39). He specifically questions norms that encourage the development of elaborate and impersonal bureaucracies and those which emphasize "mindless compliance" (p. 39) to rules or "superficial acquaintance" (p. 39) with other persons in the school environment. Furthermore, he calls teachers "to go beyond the job description and forge deep, continuous, and consistent relationships with students" (p. 39) and challenges administrators to develop policies that allow and encourage the development of caring, committed relationships.

Mitchell claims that such relationships must be achieved if other educational goals, such as improved performance or increased student engagement with learning, are to be realized.

ARGUMENTS BASED ON HISTORICAL CONCEPTIONS OF THE PURPOSES OF EDUCATION AND OF THE ROLE OF EDUCATIONAL ADMINISTRATORS

Especially in recent years, several persons have argued that ethical perspectives must be understood in light of history. Many scholars actually propose that the perspectives of the past must, in some measure, guide current thinking. Stanley Hauerwas (1981, 1983), for example, argues that ethics can be neither understood nor developed apart from their historical context. The crux of his argument is that decisions about ethical actions, "prescriptions of moral . . . conduct" (1981, p. 119), presuppose some kind of "theory of virtue [which is] necessary relative to the history of a particular community" (1981, p. 121). Hauerwas's premises are based on his understanding of the nature of ethics, for he views them not as guides to dealing with "moral quandaries" (1983, p. 4), but rather as "the convictions that tell us who we are" (1983, p. 4). He believes that people can perceive their moral identity only if they understand and recount the stories of their past. For Hauerwas, "every social ethic involves a narrative" and the truly moral community is "story-formed" (1983, p. 9).

MacIntyre (1966, 1981) also offers insights on the value of historical study in moral reasoning, suggesting that an examination of past moral thought can assist those concerned with formulating ethically sound responses to current issues. He calls upon thinkers to "allow the history of philosophy to break down present day preconceptions, so that our too narrow views of what can and cannot be thought, said, and done are discarded in face of the record of what has been thought, said, and done" (p. 4).

In turn, Dokecki (1987b) writes of the importance of historical studies for those seeking to formulate moral and effective social policy. He notes that "one important and necessary kind of useful information for judging alternatives relative to policy decision making is historical knowledge" (p. 369), and he calls upon thoughtful decision makers to consider the "historical roots" of "values, standards, and beliefs" (p. 371).

Words such as "caring" or "community" do not dominate either Dokecki's "History and Policy: A Necessary Connection" (1987b) or MacIntyre's *A Short History of Ethics* (1966). It is not, however, unreasonable to infer that both believe an examination of the past supports the importance of an ethic of caring and community building. Dokecki, in numerous other works (e.g., 1987a, 1990), suggests that effective policies will encourage "caring" (1990, p. 155), "community" (1987a, p. 90), and the development of persons whose lives demonstrate both caring and competence (Hobbs et al., 1984). And MacIntyre (1981) in *After Virtue* writes of the importance of cultivating "the virtues . . . understood as those dispositions which will not only sustain practices and enable us to achieve the good internal to practices, but which will also sustain us in the relevant kind of quest for the good" (p. 204). Furthermore, he stresses that these virtues must be pursued in the context of interdependent, communal relationships. "I am never able to seek for the good of exercise the virtues only *qua* individual" (p. 204).

Caring as Grounded in History and Tradition

Accepting the normative value of history, Bellah and his co-authors (1985) examine the roots of a commitment to caring community and factors that influence society's responses to this commitment. They suggest that a coherent sense of personal and communal identity that includes belief systems sufficient to help persons and groups make their way through difficult situations can come about only if people are aware of the stories that have formed them.

> Our lives make sense in a thousand ways, most of which we are unaware of, because of traditions that are centuries, if not millennia, old. It is these traditions that help us to know that it does make a difference who we are and how we treat one another. . . . Indeed, we would argue that if we are ever to enter that new world that so far has been powerless to be born, it will be through reversing modernity's tendency to obliterate all previous culture. We need to learn again from the cultural riches of the human species and to reappropriate and revitalize those riches so they can speak to our condition today. (pp. 282–283)

These authors believe that the fragmentation of modern life can be addressed if persons embrace an ethic that promotes interdependence and community, and they note that this requires that people become "involved in retelling [their] stories; [their] constitutive narrative[s]" (p. 153). For, in their view, these stories provide "examples of the men and women who have embodied and exemplified the meaning of the community" (p. 153). In the same vein, Hobbs and co-authors (1984) and McWilliams (1973) argue that "the ideal of a fraternal citizenry" (McWilliams, 1973, p. 219) is supported by its long philosophical history.

Bellah and co-authors (1985), Hobbs and co-authors (1984), and McWilliams (1973) all acknowledge, however, that this desire for fraternity is not the only force influencing human transactions. These authors examine, in detail, the ideological clash between "traditional moral values which have focused on community and mutuality of responsibility for individual well-being and liberal enlightenment values which emphasize political impersonality, competitions, and material power" (Hobbs et al., 1984, p. 40). In their respective works, all of these writers recognize the inevitable tensions that exist between these two value sets. They stress, though, that the enduring nature of this tension bears witness to the strength of the pull toward community.

Nisbet (1990) is another who writes, at length, of history's testimony of the inevitable movement toward community. Analyzing the many ways historical and contemporary literature, philosophy, theology, and social science reveal a "revolt against individualistic rationalism" (p. 23) and "moral aspirations toward community" (p. 26), he argues that a recurring "image of community" (p. 21) suggests that persons have an inherent need for relatedness. Indeed, he describes the "imperatives of community [as] inevitable" (p. 21). Furthermore, he asserts that "the concern for community, its values, properties, and means of access, is the major intellectual fact of the present age" (p. 26).

Another voice emphasizing that the past can serve as a moral guide for the present is Harvey Cox (1965). Focusing especially on the importance of rituals and festivals that symbolically represent and re-enact historical events, Cox uses the term *fantasy* to refer to the process by which hopes, dreams, and ethics that enable a person or a culture to respond morally to life's complex demands, grow from a celebration of historical moments. He notes that recurrent manifestations of fantasy show "man's capacity to go beyond the empirical world of the here and now. . . . In it man not only relives and anticipates, he remakes the past and creates wholly new futures" (p. 59). He further proposes that history and tradition provide guides for those seeking personal and communal development. Indeed, he describes a person progressing toward "a renaissance of the spirit" (p. 6) as one who "accepts the past without being bound by it [and views] past history not as a prison to escape or as an antique to be preserved but as a dimension of reality that enlarges and illuminates the present" (p. 32).

Caring as Supported by the History of Education

Joseph Hough (1990) argues that the purposes of education can be understood only in the light of their history and tradition. He stresses the importance of the "hermeneutics of retrieval," something he defines as "the recovery of past traditions and the appropriation of those traditions for current practice" (p. 3). In Hough's view, past traditions and current issues have a reciprocal relationship, with each informing and expanding the meaning of the other. He notes that when the current educational issues are understood in terms of past concerns, "the tradition is significantly modified by its being related to a new context for practice, but at the same time, current practice is called into account by the power of tradition" (p. 3). Hough's exegesis of historical thought about the social purposes of education is discussed at a later point in this section.

Nash (1990) and Bryk (1988), using history and tradition as rationales, suggest that schools' leaders must recognize that the creation of caring communities involves recognizing and celebrating certain values. Indeed, they propose that traditional values that support the development of individual and corporate virtues hold promise for transforming education so that positive interpersonal relationships and personal growth and development are realities for children, teachers, and administrators. In a dialogue with Robert Griffin (1990), Nash calls administrators to embrace a "communitarian world view" (p. 10). Citing Bloom (1987), he asserts that in contemporary educational thought and practice, "the individualistic principles of self-fulfillment, rights, liberty, and self-reliance have been given primacy over community, tradition, family, and nature" (p. 12). Nash argues that an appropriate commitment to community is entirely consistent with the traditional Western valuing of individualism, at least individualism in what Jeffrey Stout (1988) calls the "good sense" (p. 302). Stout defines this as the "idea that the well-being of each being, no matter how powerless or wretched or distant, should carry weight in our moral deliberation, with the burden of proof falling heavily on anyone proposing differential treatment of a sort that might place the well-being of one over that of another" (p. 302). Indeed, Nash, again drawing upon Stout, claims that this type of individualism is consistent with foundational premises of a caring ethic. He proposes that, inherent in this view, is the idea that "each of us is a worthy individual" (p. 13). Furthermore, he suggests that a belief in the basic worth of persons should lead one to a commitment to care for self and others. Nash argues that this perspective, clearly related to values of caring and community, has recurred throughout educational history and that it is an appropriate and necessary perspective for contemporary school leaders. His essay closes with a quote from Eric Springsted (1988).

> The alternative story for education is one which recognizes that larger context—the body—in which human lives are lived. It is a vision of education that does not promote community with mere words, but emphasizes the truly communal nature of education. It recognizes that communities are not only a desirable end-product of education but the context of education—whether through learning together socially and intellectually, or through conversations with thinkers and problems of the past, present, and future. This is not an unheard of story for us: it is at the root of both our biblical heritage and our Greek heritage of paideia. (Springsted, 1988, p. 154, quoted in Nash, 1990, p. 18)

Bryk (1988) asks school leaders to recognize that both inherently and traditionally education is a moral enterprise. He suggests that this recognition will lead to an enlarged vision of the purposes of education, a vision where the goals of schooling are consistent with the goals of caring. In his discussion he looks first at goals and objectives that currently dominate educational thought and then proposes ways these views might be altered so that schooling can "stimulate in students a vision of what a democratic society can be and . . . develop those abilities of mind and inculate those habits of heart that will sustain us, both individually and as a people" (p. 262). In a discussion of social studies programs, for instance, he points out that most educators are concerned "that students have a factual knowledge of our traditions" (p. 268). Instead, he recommends that administrators and teachers embrace a "more encompassing" goal, one based "in the religious and cultural traditions that have shaped our nation" (p. 264).

In Bryk's view, education should be aimed toward the development of involved, committed citizens, something that will happen only if the school is a community in which each person is considered to be a vital, contributing participant. Ultimately, he asserts that school leaders must realize that all aspects of school life must contribute to the development of "personal virtues" (p. 259) and "positive social integration" (p. 270). To that end, he recommends an examination and, possibly, a richer reconceptualization of: (1) the "craft" (p. 266) of education; (2) the ways school organization promotes a sense of community; (3) practices that foster "teacher commitment and sense of self efficacy" (p. 273); (4) factors that lead to a shared perception that "all students are valued" (p. 273); and anything that promotes the overall formation of "a predictable and nurturant environment for both students and adults who form the school community" (p. 274).

SUMMARY

Clearly, there exist a number of arguments based on beliefs about the nature of metaphysical, personal, and historical life that promote an ethic of caring in education and its administration. If an administrator accepts the premises of even some of the scholars discussed in this section—if one believes that it is consistent with the nature of God or of persons to seek caring, nurturing interactions in all of life and if one explores the strong tradition for such interactions in education—she or he, it seems, would need to consider the possibility that caring should figure strongly in administrative thought and practice. In Chapter 3 I expand the argument for an ethic of caring in educational administration by examining positions that take a more consequentialist approach to this topic. In it, I review a number of works that suggest that an ethic of caring in organizations, and specifically in schools, has real, practical benefits for both persons and institutions. I also look at the consequences that may result if such an ethic is not accepted and practiced.

3 Justifications for a Caring Ethic: Consequentialist Arguments

> . . . the school is in the best position of all U.S. institutions to initi-
> ate and strengthen links that support children and adolescents . . .
> [and] schools have the most to gain. In recent reports bemoaning
> the state of American education, a recurring theme has been the
> anomie and chaos that pervade many U.S. schools, to the detri-
> ment of effective teaching and learning. Clearly, we are in danger
> of allowing our schools to become academies of alienation.
>
> In taking the initiative, . . . U.S. schools will be taking neces-
> sary action to combat the destructive forces of alienation—first,
> within their own walls, and thereafter, in the life experience and
> future development of new generations of Americans.
> (Urie Brofenbrenner, "Alienation and the Four Worlds
> of Childhood," 1988, pp. 54–55)

The arguments for caring offered in Chapter 2 focus on the intrinsic morality of such an ethic. They emphasize that seeking to promote personal and communal growth and development is right—regardless of its outcomes. In this chapter, I examine arguments that take a different approach. Those discussed here emphasize that actions and attitudes consistent with caring are linked to observable positive outcomes in societies, organizations, and persons. Some scholars do this by taking a negative approach, noting the absence of nurturing, community-oriented actions and drawing connections between this absence and undesirable institutional or personal occurrences. Others take a positive approach as they stress that individual and corporate well-being is increased in atmospheres that emphasize personal and relational health. In this chapter, I present a number of the arguments put forward by those who focus on the outcomes, negative or positive, of the absence or presence of caring-like attitudes.

Two qualifiers are essential before I begin my discussion. The first is hinted at in my use of the word *caring-like* rather than *caring* at the end of the previous paragraph. Some of the authors I discuss stress specifically and clearly the practical importance of genuine, heartfelt concern for persons. Others focus on the results of living and working in environments where personal and interpersonal needs are either recognized or ignored. The former group generally share my understanding of a caring ethic, viewing it as the source of intentional attitudes and actions that demonstrate acceptance, nurturance, and the pursuit of personal and community development. The latter group do not seem to view intentions as being especially important. They emphasize, rather, the effects of actions—regardless of motives—that are consistent with a caring ethic. Noting that the acts they advocate may stem more from a desire to manipulate than from a commitment to care, I nevertheless include discussions offered by this group, for many of their points do support the practical importance of nurturing, person-oriented communities. Indeed, one wonders if the positive results of actions that, in some ways, appear to be caring might not increase if the actions were motivated and sustained by a genuine commitment to seek the welfare of persons and communities. A second brief qualifying statement about the arguments offered in this chapter relates to their being labeled "teleological" or consequential. As I have noted, few, if any, ethical justifications are totally deontological or totally teleological. I have elected to place certain ones in this chapter not because of their purity, but because of their emphasis on discernible results.

I begin my discussion by examining organizational outcomes related, in some way, to the lack of a caring ethos. My attention then shifts to benefits accruing to organizations whose leaders emphasize nurturing, supportive interpersonal relationships. Next, I examine effects on individual lives of the absence or presence of caring. My discussion begins with an exploration of the alienation and isolation that often characterize lives where caring is neither given nor received. I then discuss positive personal effects of involvement in nurturing relationships. In each section, the focus moves from a general discussion of consequences or benefits to an examination of this ethic's impact on schools and those who attend or work in them.

CORPORATE CONSEQUENCES OF THE ABSENCE OF CARE

Organizational or Societal Consequences

The ethical perspective that governs much modern organizational practice is one that values success reflected in the bottom line. Actions are considered good to the extent that they further profits and efficient productivity. (See Bellah et al., 1985; Bolman & Deal, 1984; Ellul, 1964; Kemp, 1970; and Kirkpatrick, 1986, for discussions of the origins of this view.) When this goal-driven, bottom-line orientation prevails, Chris Argyris (1962) suggests that a desire for "coercion and control" (p. 4) overrides a humane concern for persons. Organizational relationships suffer because "interpersonal and emotional aspects of behavior [are] suppressed" (p. 40). Further, personal development is negatively affected, for "under these conditions . . . individuals will find it very difficult to develop competence in dealing with feelings and interpersonal relationships" (p. 40). In Argyris's view, conditions such as these are related to a low level of organizational effectiveness. He notes that mistrust will characterize organizational relationships, that employees will demonstrate a low level of commitment, and that bureaucratic rigidity will discourage creative risk taking and encourage resistance to change. Although he does not actually use terms such as *caring* and *community* in his discussions, Argyris is certainly warning of the problems that result when such values are not operative. Furthermore, he does link managerial efforts to create humane organizations to certain values, including "trust, openness, . . . [and] internal commitment" (pp. 277–278), values quite in line with an ethic of care.

McGregor (1960) and Ouchi (1981) are two others who suggest that a range of organizational problems are related to impersonal (i.e., uncaring) management styles. McGregor notes that conventional management theory presupposes that lower level organizational members are naturally uncommitted to the organization and that leaders "need to actively direct and control the work of subordinates" (Bolman & Deal, 1984, p. 71, discussing McGregor, 1960). Labeling this view Theory X, McGregor believes that it produces the very attitudes it assumes, operating as a kind of self-fulfilling prophecy. Furthermore, he states that even as "the deprivation of physiological . . . [and] higher level needs" (p. 35) leads to impaired individual functioning, so the failure to meet members' needs leads to impaired organizational functioning. Ouchi (1981) relates the apparent decline of U.S. success in global economic competition to leadership styles and organizational structures that ignore the importance of persons' needs for "close, harmonious working relations" (p. 102) within institutional communities.

Several scholars, including Bellah and his co-authors (1985), Nisbet (1990), and Ellul (1964) write of the problems that occur in societies that clearly lack elements of caring communities. Bellah and co-authors describe life in a culture where goal-driven "managers and scientists" set out to create a society that is "efficient, humane, and harmonious" (p. 208). Borrowing from Tocqueville, they use the phrase "administrative despotism" (p. 208) to describe the leadership of such a society and suggest that several things can result when the goals of caring and community are ignored. For instance, they write of the possibility of "a professionalism without content . . . in the higher echelons of American society, since in the struggle to excel the practices of separation often seem to win out over the practices of commitment" (p. 210). Furthermore, they note that in social systems where "the productivity 'pay-off' is adequate, [leaders] need to think neither of the massive disparities of wealth and power in our society nor of the efforts of communities of memory to nurture ethical individuality and citizenship" (p. 210).

Nisbet (1990) uses even stronger language as he describes societies where a sense of community is ignored or denied. He writes of "a social order remote, incomprehensible, or fraudulent; beyond real hope or desire; inviting apathy, boredom, or even hostility, . . . [a society in which] the individual not only does not feel a part of the social order; he has lost interest in being a part of it" (p. xxiii). He goes on to use "such words as disorganization, disintegration, decline, insecurity, breakdown, instability, and the like" (p. 6) to underscore his view that "themes of dissolution and decay" (p. 7) dominate cultures in which "an important link is left out: the social bond, that is community" (p. xxv).

French sociologist Jacques Ellul (1964) also writes, in a despairing tone, of social and organizational conditions that relate to an intense commitment to the rational, impersonal pursuit of goals. Ellul believes that this pursuit has resulted in an unbalanced emphasis on technology and on the neglect of the basic human need for accepting, noncompetitive relationships. Furthermore, this preoccupation with the achievement of economic and efficiency goals has led persons to focus on short-term goals and to avoid asking deeper questions related to purposes behind individual and organizational relationships. Ellul believes that modern society, and organizations and persons that unquestionably accept its presuppositions are moving toward totalitarianism. He pictures organizations in the year 2000 as being under the control of "the harshest of dictatorships. [In comparison to which], Hitler's was a trifling affair. That it is to be a dictatorship of test tube rather than of hobnailed boots will not make it any less a dictatorship" (p. 434).

Educational Consequences

Ellul specifically discusses the effects of an impersonal, overly technological noncaring in schools.

> The new [rational, goal-oriented] pedagogical methods correspond exactly to the role assigned to education in modern technical society. The Napoleonic conception that the *Lycees* must furnish administrators for the state and managers for the economy, in conformity with social needs and tendencies, has become world-wide in its extent. According to this conception, education no longer has a humanist end or any value itself; it has only one goal, to create technicians. (p. 348)

By the twenty-first century, he predicts:

> Education . . . [will be] orient[ed] toward the specialized end of producing technicians; and, as a consequence, toward the creation of individuals useful only as members of a technical group—individuals who conform to the structure and the needs of the technical group, on the basis of the current criteria of utility. The intelligentsia will no longer be a model, a conscience, or an

> animating intellectual spirit for the group, even in the sense of performing a
> critical function. They will be the servants, the most conformist imaginable,
> of the instruments of technique. . . . And education will no longer be an un-
> predictable and exciting adventure in human enlightenment, but an exercise
> in conformity and an apprenticeship to whatever gadgetry is useful in a tech-
> nical world. (p. 349)

Ellul's remarks about education are offered in a philosophical vein. He does
cite some specific educational movements, such as the "techniques de l'ecole
nouvelle—progressive education" (p. 344) in his native France. He discusses
them, however, in the context of his more general indictment of "the technological society" (p. xxx). A number of educational scholars, writing more recently,
have also spoken out against organizations that focus on the efficient, rational
achievement of goals and ignore the needs of organizational members. Several
discuss, in highly specific terms, consequences of school leaders' failure to promote interdependence and community between and among administrators,
teachers, and students.

    Sedlak, Wheeler, Pullin, and Cusick (1986) write of the deleterious effects
of impersonal managerial philosophies and strategies, which have become so
prevalent in educational circles today. They describe a kind of downward cycle
that affects students' academic interest and achievement, teachers' sense of efficacy and commitment to excellence, and the emotional well-being of both
groups. Indeed, Sedlak and co-authors suggest that many of the recent reform
efforts, with their emphasis on rating and rewarding teachers on the basis of
student performance on standardized tests, place teachers at a risk of apathy,
frustration, burnout, and general disengagement from anything but the most
rudimentary commitment to their craft. Citing Lortie (1975) and Feiman-
Nemser and Floden (1986), they note that "teachers depend upon [the performance of] their students for much of their sense of success, accomplishment,
and satisfaction" (p. 99) and point out that an emphasis on externally imposed,
uniform standards tends to rob teachers of the chance to use professional dis-
cretion. Furthermore, the basic organization of schools—with a centralized
authority making decisions and monitoring the performance of employees—
isolates teachers, depriving them of opportunities to interact with other adults.
According to these authors, this situation may encourage teachers to "cultivate
and nurture good social relations in the classroom at the expense of academic
learning" (p. 100). They argue that truly effective change demands a view of
students, teachers, and parents that is consistent with a caring ethic. To that
end, they call for reforms that focus on the inherent value of persons and stress
empowerment and the cultivation of satisfying interactions among people who
have a real voice in determining the course education will follow.

    Clark and Meloy (1989) suggest that administrators who adopt impersonal, bureaucratic strategies, in essence, paralyze schools. Because such strategies do "not fit the psychological and personal needs of the work force" (p. 293), they "will never produce freedom and self-actualization" (p. 292) of organizational members. Wise (1989), Bacharach and Conley (1989), and Schlechty (1989) join Clark and Meloy in highlighting negative effects of hyper-rational impersonal school structures. The focus of these authors is the effect of such structures on faculty members. Wise suggests that teachers focus on compliance, not education, when personal and professional strengths and needs are ignored.

CORPORATE BENEFITS OF A CARING ETHOS

Organizational or Societal Benefits

Implicit in any discussion of the negative effects of a noncaring, impersonal, organizational ethos is the idea that a different kind of atmosphere—one in which participants feel they are viewed as persons, rather than as organizational resources—would have institutional benefits. Several scholars (e.g., Argyris, 1957, 1962, 1964; McGregor, 1960; Peters & Waterman, 1982) discuss ways that a human relations approach to management can enhance organizational effectiveness in the business world. A number of others (e.g., Grant, 1988; Lightfoot, 1983; Louis, 1990; Maeroff, 1990; Noddings, 1984) have written about the benefits to schools and communities of a humane, personal, caring administrative style. In this section, I look at works that emphasize positive institutional results of caring.

Underlying many human relations approaches is the work of Abraham Maslow (1970), who argues that persons are motivated by a hierarchy of needs. As physiological and safety needs are met, psychological and emotional needs assume a prominent place in motivating human behavior. Argyris (1957, 1962, 1964) and McGregor (1960), building upon Maslow's work, offer theories and empirical data supporting the importance—in terms of organizational outputs—of administrative actions that address such issues as the need to experience loving relationships with others, the need to feel valued and important, and the need to feel efficacious.

Argyris (1962) reports the results of a study in which executives who held traditional management values were given "laboratory training" (p. 283) to develop their relational skills. Various organizational changes that seemed to be related to changes in management style were noted, and the employee attitudes in experimental groups were compared with those in a control group. Argyris notes that data revealed "increases in such qualities as openness, trust, confidence, and decreases in conformity, crises, fear, and conflict" (p. 279) in the experimental group. These changes, in his view, are attributable to humane, relationally oriented management, and he argues that "the basic values which emphasize the dignity and importance of the individual can be integrated with the fury and pressure of everyday administrative life to the benefit of the individual and the organization" (p. 279).

McGregor (1960) and Ouchi (1981) argue, from a theoretical perspective, that administrators who recognize and respond to employee needs for recognition, a sense of efficacy and ownership, and satisfying interpersonal relationships will elicit high levels of production and commitment. McGregor (1960) sums up these concepts in what he calls Theory Y. At the heart of this theory is the idea that "the essential task of management is to arrange organizational conditions so that people can achieve their own goals best by directing their efforts toward organizational rewards" (p. 61). Using slightly different terms, Ouchi (1981) suggests that traditional organizational strategies and those embodied in McGregor's Theory Y consider employees as resources to be manipulated by leaders for the good of the organization. He argues that a true reconceptualization of organizational purposes that includes "a commitment to . . . people . . . [and] developing inter-personal skills" (Bolman & Deal, 1984, p. 102, discussing Ouchi) will result in a transformed organization with increased effectiveness and efficiency. To support this view, Ouchi (1981) points to the success of Japanese business organizations and suggests that this is related to a focus on "humanized working conditions . . . [increasing] the self-esteem for employees . . . [and] a redirection of attention to human relations in the corporate world" (p. 165).

Educational Benefits

Numerous works, some theoretical or philosophical and some empirical, testify to the fact that schools—perhaps even more than businesses—flourish under leadership that stresses cooperation, acceptance, nurturance, and interdependence. A large body of research on cooperative learning suggests that the academic performance of students—especially low-performing students—improves when educators stress cooperation rather than competition. After reviewing more than 70 studies in which outcomes of cooperative learning groups were compared with those of traditional classes, Neil Davidson (1989) reports that more than 40% of the cooperative groups outperformed other groups and that only two studies reported higher performance from those receiving traditional instruction. Davidson's work focuses especially on the effects of this teaching style on mathematics learning. Other studies that support the relationships between improved math scores and cooperative learning include ones by Slavin and Madden (1989) and Treisman (1986). Johnson, Johnson, Holobee, and Roy (1984) note that the academic benefits of this method are by no means limited to math.

Slavin, one of the chief proponents of interdependent, noncompetitive teaching and learning, points out that an overall improvement in academic scores, something equated by many as the production focus of schools, is only one of many benefits that result from a concomitant stress on relationships and learning. In *Cooperative Learning* (1983), he reports that students who participated in group learning reported more and more lasting cross-racial friendships than did those in control groups. Aljose and Joyner (1990), commenting on this result, state, "Given the heterogeneous nature of our society and the urgent need for various ethnic groups to get along, this social consequence of cooperative learning may ultimately be as important as its academic benefits" (p. 201). Clearly, administrators who support cooperative learning methods are not necessarily caring leaders. However, the chief tenets of this pedagogical strategy

—positive interdependence . . .
—promotive interaction . . .
—the frequent use of interpersonal skills . . .
—engagement in periodic and regular group processing (Aljose & Joyner, 1990, p. 198)

are remarkably congruent with key aspects of an ethic of care. It is not illogical to surmise that administrators who support cooperative learning or other teaching methods that deemphasize individual competition and stress supportive interpersonal relationships would accept and possibly exhibit some degree of caring in their leadership.

One of the distinctive qualities of cooperative learning is a focus on the affective experiences of students. Beane (1990), writing about effective middle schools, emphasizes that educators most successful in teaching young adolescents are those who "provide more balanced response to the physical, cognitive, and affective aspects of learning and development" (p. 109). This balance usually requires "sustained attention" (p. 109) to the emotional needs of middle schoolers. Many of his statements about the philosophy and attitudes of effective middle school administrators suggest that those committed to caring relationships are most likely to lead schools that work successfully with young people in all areas. Regarding the philosophical orientation of effective leaders, Beane writes:

Beyond academics and coping skills, we should want to help young adolescents to be fully functioning human beings. [Furthermore,] affective development involves more than self-esteem; it includes social as well as personal development. . . . Thus, efforts to extend affective dimensions of a middle school must also address values, morals, ethics, and other aspects of our relations with others. (p. 110)

Although Beane does not use the word *caring,* this perspective is certainly the type one would expect from caring leaders. He offers a number of specific suggestions regarding actions caring educators might take (some of which are discussed in Chapter 5). What is of interest at this point is Beane's linkage of a school's general effectiveness to its success in addressing social and personal needs. He labels the idea that "affective and cognitive learning and development are unrelated," a "historical mistake" (p. 111) and states that a concern with creating a nurturing school atmosphere should be an important goal of educators.

Kohut's (1990) article on quality middle schools supports the view expressed by Beane. That is, adults in excellent schools feel a concern for the total development of students and act to create an environment that nurtures this development. To explain this perspective, Kohut notes that a "flexible curriculum [that] provides continuous assessment of individual students' needs" (p. 107) is an important feature and that, in quality schools, concern with academic success is not overshadowed by concern for "the total life of the student" (p. 108). Furthermore, Kohut stresses that, in such schools, a sense of community and interdependence is present as principals share responsibilities and privileges with both teachers and students.

A descriptive report by Gene Maeroff (1990) supports Kohut's assertions. After conducting an in-depth observation of a middle school "cited as exemplary in *Turning Points,* the report of the Carnegie Corporation's Task Force on Education of Young Adolescents" (p. 506), Maeroff notes several characteristics that seem, at least in this case, to be related to a record of high scholastic achievement and community satisfaction. Several of his comments point to a caring atmosphere, which, in his view, is related to the school's overall success. He notes that "Shoreham-Wading River relies on the quality of human interactions, not on the building or the campus to shape its character" (p. 507). This emphasis has led to structures in which "the sense of community for students and teachers" (p. 507) thrives, and "close bonds are encouraged and competition is discouraged" (p. 509).

Maeroff suggests that this supportive atmosphere, with its stress on nurturing, positive, interpersonal relationships, is linked both to teacher commitment and to student achievement in this school. Furthermore, he notes that the principal's attitude is a key to maintaining this cycle of benefits. On the subject of teacher attitude and effectiveness, he writes:

> The faculty is surely the linchpin of Shoreham-Wading River's attempt to build a community that wraps its warm, supportive arms around the children. "The principal hired us 17 years ago," said Jerry Silverstein, who teaches theater and film. "He had a strong philosophy and involved the staff in almost all decisions." (p. 509)

On the issue of student academic achievement, he offers the following impressive data:

> It should be noted that last spring the school's average seventh-grader exceeded the national average on the Stanford Achievement Test by a full two years in math and a full three years in reading. And this is a school in which the average I.Q. score is only 112. Whatever their scholastic achievement, students from the middle school by and large reach ninth grade with a favorable attitude toward school. "They come to us confident and not afraid to take chances," said Carol Willen, an administrator at Shoreham-Wading River High School, which draws its entire enrollment of 700 from this one middle school. (pp. 509–510)

Maeroff implies that the supportive, involved attitudes within this school have extended to the larger community, especially to the parents of students enrolled at Shoreham-Wading River. Sharon Elder (1990), reporting on the work of James Comer in New Haven, Connecticut, also suggests that administrative action that focuses on individual and interpersonal growth and development, can result in measurable, positive outcomes in schools. Comer's basic premise is that "a working partnership among the school staff, the students, and their families . . . [can result] in an emotional bond" (p. 50) between these groups and in a shared commitment to work toward the well-being of the school and of its students. Consistent with a caring ethic's emphasis on interpersonal interactions, Comer's programs stress meeting emotional and relational needs before turning attention to the achievement of academic success. In the two main sites for implementing Comer's program students' academic achievement (as measured by standardized test scores) and attendance have steadily increased. Writers describing these phenomena (e.g., Elder, 1990; Schorr, 1989) suggest that the caring ethos within these schools has undoubtably contributed to these improvements.

Lightfoot (1983) offers compelling pictures of six very different schools, all of which, in her estimation, are good schools. In examining themes that seem to run through these schools, Lightfoot notes two that suggest the pervasiveness of a caring ethos that begins with the school's leaders. She points out that "the fearless and empathetic regard of students" (p. 342) is evident in all of these institutions. Furthermore, she notes that "students evidence a loyalty, belonging, and responsibility in the membership" (p. 349) and that the organizations demonstrate interest in all students but especially a "concern for saving lost souls and helping students who are most vulnerable" (p. 349). Her statement, "Good schools are places where students are seen as people worthy of respect" (p. 350), succinctly summarizes this point. A second highlighted characteristic relates to the leadership style of principals in these schools. Lightfoot reports that all the principals, even those who fit many "masculine" stereotypes, make an effort to incorporate both masculine and feminine qualities into their administrative style. Recognizing their "need for partnership and nurturance" (p. 333), these leaders actively cultivate caring relationships with teachers, students, and parents.

Descriptions of quality schools by Grant (1988) support the idea that one dimension of good schools is a caring principal. Grant describes changes that occurred at Robert W. Cook High School after Joseph Conan assumed the principalship. The magnitude of these changes is evident only if one first understands the status of Cook when Conan entered his leadership role.

> When Conan was called back to the school as principal in 1976, he found that vandalism was high, thefts from school lockers were averaging $350 a week. Teacher morale was low, drug use was widespread, and absenteeism had increased. (p. 196).

As principal, he did not adopt a "mere law-and-order approach" (p. 196). Instead he focused on ways the entire school could become more of a community where respect for others grew out of caring relationships between its members.

> Conan was unashamed to talk to the faculty about "love of mankind" or to ask, "If we are not here to serve people, what else is there in life?" He visited students in the hospital and took school-work to the homes of those who had been suspended to show that discipline was not born of hatred. He had the capacity to engage the students, faculty, and parents in dialogue about issues that really mattered. (p. 197)

Numerous positive changes occurring under Conan suggest a link between a caring environment and educational excellence. "Student achievement increased under Conan even as vandalism, littering, stealing, drug use, and other kinds of negative behavior decreased. Most impressive, though, was the effect of Conan's leadership on teacher satisfaction" (p. 201).

Amplifying the points made by Grant, a number of thinkers stress that efforts to increase the overall effectiveness of schools must concentrate on factors that improve teachers' sense of commitment, efficacy, and satisfaction (Lortie, 1975; Rosenholtz & Simpson, 1990). Ashton and Webb in *Making a Difference: Teachers' Sense of Efficacy and Student Achievement* (1986) discuss various research efforts that support links between educators' sense of commitment and satisfaction; supportive, collegial interactions among teachers and administrators; opportunities for caring, personal involvement with students; student achievement; and organizational effectiveness. For example, they cite studies by Ellett and Masters (1978), Meyer and Cohen (1971), and Little (1982) that suggest that "school structures that enhance teachers' opportunities for collegial interaction have a positive effect on teachers' attitudes and student performance" (p. 19).

Ashton and Webb also suggest that caring, supportive, personal actions on the part of principals—toward teachers and students—are related to organizational effectiveness. Citing Chapman and Lowther (1982), they note that "one aspect of the principal's role that is likely to be related to teachers' sense of efficacy is the principal's recognition and support of teachers" (p. 19). Additionally, Ashton and Webb discuss the results of Leithwood and Montgomery's (1982) extensive review of research on principals in successful elementary schools. Some of this review's findings are clearly supportive of a relationship between caring leaders and school effectiveness. For instance, Leithwood and Montgomery found that "in terms of goals, the first priority of effective principals was the achievement and happiness of their students" (Ashton & Webb, 1986, p. 20). This suggests that effective schools tend to be led by administrators who have a deep concern for students' holistic, personal development.

INDIVIDUAL CONSEQUENCES OF THE ABSENCE OF CARE

Consequences Affecting All Individuals

The presence or absence of caring interactions appears to be related to some observable organizational occurrences. In the same way, participation, or the lack thereof, in nurturing, supportive relationships seems to be related to some outcomes in individual lives. In this section, I discuss some apparent effects of the absence of caring occurring on a personal, rather than institutional, level. As I offer this discussion, I am again aware that I am making distinctions that are somewhat artificial. Individual and organizational outcomes related to caring or noncaring clearly are linked. My decision to categorize justifications or arguments is, therefore, not intended to suggest that I view these as discrete phenomena. Rather, it reflects my understanding of the dominant emphasis of various discussions.

Two works that present vivid pictures of lives where caring and commitment are noticeably absent are Keniston's *The Uncommitted* (1965) and Bellah and colleagues' *Habits of the Heart* (1985). These works present vivid pictures of alienated, isolated individuals whose lives are, in many ways, defined by the absence of attachment to others. In both, the authors go beyond description and attempt to trace the etiology of this lack of commitment. Keniston presents the results of an extensive "study with a group of alienated young men . . . [a group for whom] alienation is more than a vague sense of estrangement, though it is that. It is also a way of life" (p. 8). He opens by writing about one of these men, who "stand[s] as a prototypically alienated young man" (p. 25). Using vivid images, he describes this man as

> separated by his own volition from the people, institutions, and beliefs which sustain most young men at his age in America, condemned like the Biblical Ishmael by his past and by Melville's Ishmael by his own temper to live on the outskirts of society. (p. 25)

Keniston suggests that the extreme emotional isolation of this "American Ishmael" (p. 23) is related to early experiences where genuine caring was, in large measure, withheld. This young man's mother was viewed by her son as "'a rather possessive person'; obviously a strong figure, 'not quite like the cat who swallowed the canary' but rather supercilious towards [her child]" (p. 35). Keniston also uses words such as "engulfed" and "clutches" in discussing mother/child interactions. The father was absent from his son's life for a four-year period of military service. Commenting on him, the young man stated, "'The father, being absent, sort of leaves him out of my mind'" (p. 39). Keniston believes that these early experiences played a clear role in the later alienation of the son. He further notes that most of the alienated young men he studied had similar perceptions of their childhood relationships. Typically, they reported close relationships with mothers who apparently sought to meet some of their own unmet desires in dominating, controlling relationships with their sons. The sons also, generally, reported a low level of paternal care and involvement. Keniston is quick to acknowledge that other factors, both individual and environmental, also seemed to contribute to the alienation of those he studied. For example, he writes of the typically American values of independence, success, and hard work and of the values that emerged with such strength in the 1960s, such as distrust of established authority and disillusionment with materialism. In his view, a lack of healthy parental nurturance, conflicts in beliefs and values, and the temperaments of the alienated young men combined to produce, in his subjects, "alienation, estrangement, disaffection, anomie, withdrawal, disengagement, separation, non-involvement, apathy, indifference, and neutralism" (p. 3).

Bellah and his colleagues (1985) also look at the cultural and ideological roots of alienation and isolation in modern America. Their discussion, like Keniston's, suggests a link between a sense of atomism and aloneness and the absence of caring, nurturing communities. Noting "a sense of fragmentariness" (p. 277) in the lives of persons they interviewed, Bellah and colleagues propose that a misunderstanding of the intentions of America's founders regarding individualism, rights, independence, the purpose of work, and self-expression, and a fundamental loss of a sense of community membership have combined to create—in many—a sense that they are in competition with others and that they must evaluate each of their actions and relationships as to whether they further or diminish chances to win in this competition.

Brofenbrenner (1988) chooses the word "alienation" (p. 52) to describe the lives of children who fail to enjoy caring relationships within supportive communities. The lives of these children are characterized by stress. This, however, "is not the main danger. What threatens the well-being of children and young people the most is that the external havoc can become internal, first for parents and then for children" (p. 53). In his view, such conditions can lead to personal alienation and a blockage in natural, desirable human development.

Similar ideas are expressed by Erik Erikson (1968), who suggests that development requires persons to "grow by epigenetic steps through psychosocial crises" (p. 222). In his view, these crises present certain developmental tasks that must be accomplished if psychological maturation is to proceed. "The human environment as a whole must permit and safeguard a series of more or less discontinuous and yet culturally and psychologically consistent developments, each extending further along the radius of expanding life tasks" (p. 221). A large number of these tasks require that developing individuals give or receive care. If opportunities to do so are absent from a person's life, then healthy development is stymied. Instead of passing from an infancy of trust—through a young adulthood where intimate relationships are established and into maturity with a sense of generativity of giving to others—a person will experience distrust, isolation, and a sense of stagnation and personal futility.

The experiences of persons living in a world where caring is absent have also been vividly portrayed in literature, art, and music. One of the most dramatic examples is contained in Mary Shelley's classic *Frankenstein* (1981, originally published 1818). In this tale, Victor Frankenstein, aspiring to understand and to control life and death, "create[s] a rational creature" (p. 199). As soon as this creature draws his first breath, Frankenstein is overwhelmed with a sense of abhorrence. Throughout the story, the creature seeks, alternatively, love and companionship and, when these are denied him, revenge. In the moments where he pursues love, the creature begs his Frankenstein to make a companion for him so that he can experience some kind of relatedness. In his moments of revenge, he brutally kills everyone dear to his creator. Throughout the novel, Frankenstein not only refuses to care, in any way, for the one he has made, but actually takes action to bring about the creature's destruction. These harsh and hostile interactions control and ultimately destroy both Frankenstein and the one he had made. After the death of his creator and before his own demise, the creature utters words that dramatically portray the inner reality of being completely uncared for. In the presence of Frankenstein's body, the creature, speaking to a ship captain, says:

> My heart was fashioned to be susceptible to love and sympathy, and when wrenched by misery to vice and hatred, it did not endure the violence of the

change without torture such as you cannot imagine. Even that enemy of God and man had friends and associates in his desolation; I am alone. (pp. 203–204)

The inner and outer destruction of this creature and of his creator vividly depicts the intense pain of those who neither give nor receive care.

Consequences for Individuals in Educational Settings

Some scholars have focused specifically on student and teacher outcomes apparently linked to uncaring educational atmospheres. Elkind (1981, 1984) writes of the sense of depersonalization in schools where "success of schools [is measured] not by the kinds of human beings they promote but by whatever increase in reading scores they chalk up" (Keniston, 1976, in Elkind, 1981, p. 53). Such schools achieve by "ignoring individual differences" (1981, p. 38) and, in Elkind's view, rob children of chances to learn and grow in a healthy, productive way.

Powell, Farrar, and Cohen's *The Shopping Mall High School* (1985) also provides insight into the effects of an impersonal educational system on many students. They especially condemn the way educators, in an effort to accommodate and process large numbers with minimal trouble, have redefined education's purposes. In their view, simply getting students through—not encouraging maximal development—is the goal that drives many programs. The students who suffer in this type of system are labeled as "the unspecial" (p. 172). These are the academically average who make little trouble, do enough to meet minimum requirements, and move through school taking little away from the experience and giving little to either the school or other people. Some points made by these authors regarding the plight of these students are especially worthy of note because they emphasize the differences between stereotypically caring actions and caring actions as defined in this book. Powell and co-authors note that "self-proclaimed average students [think] that friendly and tolerant relationships [are] the most important thing about high school" (p. 191). At first glance, it might seem as if these students are describing caring interactions. However, closer examination of these students' experiences suggests that a commitment to human development within communities is not motivating educators. Teachers and administrators within the schools described by Powell and his co-authors apparently are motivated by a desire to pass students through their schools and classes with a minimum amount of disruption. Superficial tolerance and friendliness become substitutes for caring commitments to the total well-being of others, and the results are general apathy, disengagement from learning, low expectations, and concomitant low achievement.

Students apparently are not the only persons who suffer in impersonal, uncaring schools. Many who write about the experiences of adults—teachers and administrators—note the occurrence of apathy, frustration, and a sense of compromising their professional and personal aspirations when educators are blocked from caring, supportive interactions with students and with fellow professionals (see, e.g., Grant, 1988; Rosenholtz & Simpson, 1990; Silberman, 1970; Sizer, 1985). Reporting on an extensive study of workplace conditions and teacher perceptions, Rosenholtz and Simpson (1990) stress that bureaucratic policies that fail to recognize and value teachers as competent, contributing professionals correlate with low levels of teacher satisfaction and commitment. Sizer (1985), writing on the experiences of Horace, the archetypal career educator, expresses similar views. He describes the wearing down of a teacher who must contend with standardized, bureaucratic policies and working conditions that ignore the individual, personal needs and strengths of students and teachers. Sizer's title, with its stress on compromise, points to one of the key consequences of impersonal, uncaring schools. That is, teachers find themselves compromising their professional standards and integrity as they struggle to meet the many demands placed on them by a powerful and demanding system.

A novel that explores the inner world of an adolescent who, ostensibly, cares for very few people and, obviously, does not feel cared for by his family, teachers, or fellow students is J. D. Salinger's (1951) *The Catcher in the Rye*. When the novel opens, Holden Caulfield, the protagonist, has been "kicked . . . out" (p. 4) of Pencey Prep and has responded by cynically disengaging himself from his environment. As the novel progresses, Holden's cynicism grows. One pivotal point in the development of his alienation comes when he is disillusioned by a former favorite teacher. Holden believes that Mr. Antolini is one of the rare teachers who really cares about him, a fact that makes this man, in Holden's view, "about the best teacher I ever had" (p. 174). As the two of them spend more time together, Antolini makes what Holden considers to be homosexual overtures. Not only does he reject Mr. Antolini, but Holden Caulfield also rejects the belief that he himself is worthy of respect and that seeking an education is one way for him to care for himself. By the end of the novel, Caulfield's cynicism seems to be entrenched. Visiting a museum where the tombs of pharaohs are displayed, he reflects on life.

> I was the only one left in the tomb then. I sort of liked it, in a way. It was so nice and peaceful. Then all of a sudden, you'd never guess what I saw on the wall. Another "Fuck you." It was written with a red crayon or something right under the glass part of the wall, under the stone.
>
> That's the whole trouble. You can't ever find a place that's nice and peaceful, because there isn't any. You may think there is, but once you get there, when you're not looking, somebody'll sneak up and write "Fuck you" right under your nose. Try it sometime. I think even, if I ever die, and they stick me in a cemetery, and I have a tombstone and all, it'll say "Holden Caul-

field" on it, and then what year I was born and when I died, and then right under that it'll say "Fuck you." I'm positive, in fact. (p. 202)

This cynicism and the alienation and lack of commitment it represents apparently are common in the lives of those deprived of the opportunity to give or receive care.

INDIVIDUAL BENEFITS OF GIVING AND RECEIVING CARE

Scholarly and imaginative literature is replete with evidence that care, given and received, brings much that is good into the lives of persons. In this section, I explore some of this evidence. As in earlier sections, I open with an examination of some of the more general correlates of caring personal interactions. I then focus specifically on benefits in the lives of those who study and work in caring schools.

General Benefits for Individuals

Receiving some measure of care is, according to many, as basic to life and health as air, food, and water. Physician Willard Gaylin in *Caring* (1976) offers an overview of scholarship that suggests that humans have a basic need for nurturance, which must be satisfied if growth and development are to proceed. He refers to Freud (1926) who spoke of the biological helplessness and dependence of the human infant and stated, "This biological factor, then, established the earliest situation of danger and creates the need to be loved which will accompany the child through the rest of its life" (quoted on p. 28). Gaylin also refers to Harlow's (1958, 1961) work with animals and to Bowlby's (1952, 1958, 1969, 1973) studies of human infants to emphasize that a nurturant bond between an infant and a care giver is essential for later development. "It is necessary to be loved in a specific caring way. It is being loved in this way that initiates in the child the capacity to give love to others" (pp. 62–63).

In a similar manner, Fromm (1956), Mayeroff (1971), and Noddings (1984) write of the vital ways involvement in caring relationships contributes to personal well-being. Fromm stresses that this involvement protects persons from being overwhelmed by negative feelings. In his view, *"The awareness of human separation, without reunion by love—is the source of shame. It is at the same time the source of guilt and anxiety"* (p. 8, emphasis in original). Fromm's rather bleak assessment of the human condition is balanced by his optimistic view that loving relationships can mitigate these harmful inner states. These interactions replace shame, guilt, and anxiety with security, a sense of belonging, and a belief that each person has value because of her/his personhood.

Mayeroff (1971) views caring as an ethical perspective that enables persons to order their lives, choosing between alternative courses of action because of commitment to the welfare of self and others. This ordering, in his view, offers numerous psychological benefits:

> Caring then provides a center around which my activities and experiences are integrated. This results in a harmonizing of the self with the world that is deep-seated and enduring. . . . This deep-seated harmony of self with the world is distinct from passively accommodating ourselves to the world or from trying to subject the world to our will. (p. 38)

He also notes that caring brings stability to life, a quality described by Mayeroff as being "in-place." He defines this concept as the experience of "rest [that] is dynamic rather than static" (p. 40) "in some kind of harmony with one another" (p. 4). For Noddings (1984), caring provides an axis for ethical decision making. Indeed, she argues that persons experience maximal moral development only if they, in attitudes and actions, seek the growth and development of others and of themselves. Noddings suggests that moral maturity results in an affective state characterized by "joy, wonder, engagement, and tenderness" (p. 174).

Bellah and co-authors (1985) write of another benefit that comes to persons who live and interact within caring communities. This is the lifting of a sense of pressure that one must constantly work to earn her or his place in a social system. They note that typical modern ethical perspectives encourage a belief that value lies in one's achievement. Those who hold this view, regardless of their personal level of success, live in a state of personal insecurity. If they have attained a certain level of achievement, they must constantly strive to maintain it; if they have not achieved, they must work to attain success. Persons who hold this perspective evaluate their lives on the basis of their achievements. Their sense of worth is conditional on meeting some external standard of value. For those who hold a caring ethic, the value of lives, their own and others', has a very different basis. They believe persons possess inherent worth and dignity. A caring, community-oriented ethic frees persons from pressuring others and themselves to constantly strive to earn or maintain value.

Benefits to Individuals in Educational Settings

Bellah and colleagues (1985) suggest that the presence of this ethic in schools could have a strong, positive impact in the lives of students and educators. They argue that caring educational communities have the potential to "provide the meaning and love that make competitive striving bearable" (p. 292). These authors propose that curricula can and should focus on reminding students that they are members of communities where the value of persons rests not upon achievement, but upon shared humanity. They also note that school policies and educator actions can, "in Christopher Jencks's [1972] words, . . . reduce the 'punishments of failure and the rewards of success' [p. 8]" (p. 287). Surely, this would encourage creative thinking and risk taking on the part of the students, teachers, and administrators. Reuben Fine (1985) also agrees that personal creativity is related to involvement in loving relationships. He writes, "Creativity involves the capacity to work, while the loss of creativity betrays an underlying depression. And in all of them love is the motor that makes the wheels turn" (p. 336).

Margaret Buchmann (1989) discusses the impact this type of creativity has on teachers' personal and professional lives. She proposes that "contemplative thinking" (p. 35) provides a base from which teachers can make creative decisions regarding materials and methods and can gain deep and useful understanding of themselves, their students, and colleagues. Buchmann relates this kind of thinking to caring in two ways. She suggests that an antecedent of such thought is a commitment to seek moral, growth-inducing pedagogical strategies. When teachers possess this commitment, their thought will take on a quality Hannah Arendt (1978) describes as "an admiring wonder" (p. 143, quoted on p. 38), and "thinking [will be linked] with the claims of the heart; as Wordsworth wrote, 'Tis still the hour of thinking, feeling, loving'" (p. 38). Buchmann argues that contemplation is a central factor in developing teachers' abilities to practice their profession in a considerate, service-oriented manner. Indeed, she emphasizes that thinking and moral virtue are intertwined and that, together, they enable persons to engage in acts of caring service. This, in her view, is essential to excellent teaching.

Johnson (1987) is another who suggests a link between caring and excellence in teaching. In her view, teachers who believe that they are recognized, valued, and cared for will, generally, be productive and effective. She writes, "In order for [teachers] to give their best they must be aware of their strengths and the confidence others have in them" (p. 3). Furthermore, she proposes that this confidence is most readily conveyed in schools where administrators are "caring, trusting, and supportive" (p. 4) of teachers. Schaps and Solomon (1990) note that teachers are not the only persons who benefit from a caring environment. Describing the Child Development Project in two California districts, they state that efforts to create "a caring community within each school and each classroom" (p. 38) are linked to increases in students' social and academic development. Schaps and Solomon especially credit "close, stable relationships with caring adults" (p. 40) as being pivotal in these developmental improvements. These relationships provide "feeling[s] of belonging and contributing" (p. 39), which provide the foundation for children's "intellectual, social, and moral" (p. 38) growth.

Concurring with Schaps and Solomon, Mitchell (1990a) emphasizes that a sense of belonging is a prerequisite for "'healthy' human development" (p. 19). He focuses especially on the ways social policy allows and encourages an educational atmosphere conducive to a sense of secure community membership. Challenging the economic metaphors that have dominated educational policies in recent years, Mitchell calls on administrators to consider embracing images that reflect a commitment to "mutual growth and development" rather than "survival and self-interest" (p. 42). He believes that policies inspired by and communicating this commitment offer the only real hope for the transformation of schools into places where persons "acquire durable self-esteem, flexible and inquiring habits of mind, reliable and relatively close human relationships, a sense of belonging in a valued group and a sense of usefulness in some way beyond self" (Carnegie Council, 1989, p. 12, quoted on p. 45).

SUMMARY

The discussions in this and the preceding chapter were not offered in an attempt to "prove" that caring should be an administrative ethic or activity. Rather, my goal was to bring together a set of arguments that, at the least, justify the legitimacy of exploring the possibility that this ethic might be right and useful for school leaders. In this chapter, I specifically focus on the usefulness of caring, contending that schools where this ethical perspective influences culture, interactive behaviors, organizational structures, and the like, are more likely to be places where students learn, teachers teach, and persons and communities flourish. In the following chapters, I narrow my focus a bit and look at the impact a caring ethic can and should have on administrators as they face the multiple and complex challenges of school leadership.

4 Meeting Future Challenges: The Place of a Caring Ethic

> . . . the criticism of present-day administrators and their prepara-
> tion are loud and clear and the demand for reform is heard on all
> sides.
> (Daniel Griffiths, *Educational Administration: Reform PDQ or RIP,*
> 1988, p. 8)

Educational leaders today are bombarded by demands—from government officials, parents, teachers, students, and colleagues within their own profession.
These demands represent important and valid concerns; they also, though, represent divergent perspectives on education's purposes and on the role of administrators in fulfilling these purposes. This divergence, coupled with the urgency
with which many of these challenges are presented, tends to drive practice in
different, conflicting directions. Indeed, conscientious school officers are likely
to find themselves rushing from one crisis to another, taking action to quell the
more obvious or serious problems before moving on to other issues. Clearly,
what is needed is an organizing perspective, an understanding of education and
leadership, which can assist leaders in sifting through and prioritizing demands
and in making wise decisions regarding their actions and responses.

I propose that an ethic of caring has the potential to provide a solid foundation for such a perspective and, in this chapter, offer arguments supporting this
position. I do so by identifying and discussing three pivotal challenges that dominate discussions of tasks facing educators as we move toward the twenty-first
century (see, e.g., Beck & Murphy, 1993; Cuban, 1988; Mitchell & Cunningham, 1990; Murphy, 1991). These are: (1) administering schools in ways that
result in improved performances—of students and teachers; (2) addressing a
host of social problems within and through schools; and (3) rethinking organizational structures so that schools will be better able to meet the preceding challenges. As I discuss each, I identify a model of schooling that has, in my view,
been especially influential in the usual conceptualization of the challenge and
in our development of strategies to address it. As a part of this, I examine values,
beliefs, and ethical perspectives embedded in the various models and go on
to assert that each model, with its attendant ethical preferences, has certain
shortcomings. After a brief discussion of these inadequacies, I then look at ways

an ethic of caring and an ecological model of schools complement and complete other perspectives.

CHALLENGE ONE: IMPROVING ACADEMIC PERFORMANCE

Influence of an Economic Model

Since the early 1980s, educational administrators have been bombarded by calls for excellence in schools (for an overview, see Toch, 1991). Implicit in these calls is a strong production emphasis. Educational leaders are repeatedly called on to focus on the goal of producing students who can function effectively and successfully in the workplace. Embedded in this challenge is a certain understanding of schooling, an understanding that includes assumptions about the primary purposes of education and the best and most appropriate way to achieve those purposes. Most who hold that producing an educated workforce is the chief challenge for school leaders assume that an economic model provides an appropriate framework for analyzing educational problems and developing solutions. This model's influence is especially evident in discussions of education's goals and purposes and in recommendations regarding ways to move schools toward excellence.

Especially in recent years, the assumption that the primary purpose of education is to prepare young people to enter successfully into the world of work has permeated discussions of schooling in the United States. (See, e.g., Martin, 1990; National Governors' Association, 1986; Shea, 1990.) Some, writing in this vein, define successful entry in terms of the achievement of high levels of personal status and income and argue that schools should focus on equipping individual students to compete against others in the quest for these resources. Others emphasize the school's duty to provide to large groups of students the basic skills needed in the workplace. Differing slightly in their views on the deepest purposes of education—the former emphasizing the promotion of individual achievement, and the latter, the development of group competency—these thinkers share, however, two assumptions. First, they tend to define the school's mission in economic terms. In their view, education should have as a central goal the efficient production of persons who possess "the strong skills needed to find and keep a good job" (Lamar Alexander, quoted in National Governors' Association, 1986, p. 7). Second, persons writing in this vein assume that schools have a direct effect on national and global economies. Positing causal links between school leadership, educational quality, students' acquisition of knowledge, and the economic health of our country, they blame educational administrators for many problems occurring in this chain. (See Murphy, 1992, for a review of this type of reasoning.)

Exemplifying this perspective, the National Education Association, in 1983, claimed, "As the economy becomes increasingly dependent on information and new technologies, we will not be able to compete effectively unless the basic skills of the labor force improve" (p. 29). This organization then called on its members to concentrate on improving technological expertise to prepare students for the twenty-first-century workplace. Five years later, David Kearnes asserted that this had not happened. "Public education has put this country at a terrible competitive disadvantage. The American work force is running out of qualified people" (1988a, p. 566).

Solutions proposed to respond to these warnings and criticisms also reflect the influence of an economic model in that they concentrate on increasing the quality and quantity of inputs into education under the assumption that more and better outputs will result. The American Association of School Administrators (1985), for example, calls for raising standards and expectations, for an increased emphasis on basic skills (i.e., a core curriculum) with a concomitant deemphasis on extracurricular and elective activities, for more class time devoted to instruction and greater amounts of homework to supplement classwork, and for higher and stricter standards for teacher certification and performance. The National School Board Association (1984) focuses on similar reforms. Others emphasize improving teacher and administrator preparation programs (Council for Chief State School Officers, 1989; National Governors' Association, 1986); changing the type and amounts of preservice and inservice training (Gage, 1989; Psyzkowski, 1988); devising incentives to attract and retain quality personnel (National Education Association, 1983; Schlechty, 1989; United States Department of Education, 1984); improving administrator–teacher relationships (Ashton & Webb, 1986; Bacharach & Conley, 1989; Wise, 1989); and developing more effective monitoring and evaluative methods (Bridges, 1988; Council for Chief State School Officers, 1989; United States Department of Education, 1984).

A Competitive Ethic and an Economic Model

Consistent with the free market ideology that they tend to embrace, proponents of an economic model of schools look to a competitive ethic as that most able to guide school leaders in achieving production goals. Brinelow's (1985) claim is exemplary of this view: "Public education has been a curious and anomalous experiment with socialism. Its problems will remain chronic until it is exposed to competition" (p. 347).

Discussing the pervasiveness of a competitive perspective, Shea (1990) claims that marketplace ethics have influenced numerous educational policies. Drawing upon Wilson's (1987) comments on the words of former Secretary of

Education William Bennett, she offers evidence that competition was an accepted guide in educational policy formation during the Reagan–Bush years.

> Throughout his administration, Secretary of Education William Bennett has reiterated time and again that federal level, liberal-style programs and spending are not the key to boosting America's economic competitiveness. According to Bennett, "Gimmicky programs or new labels aren't going to make us more competitive—any more than new uniforms will make a football team play better. . . . The roots of competitiveness lie in the character of our people." (Wilson, 1987, p. 29, cited in Shea, 1990, p. 21)

Shea argues that policies formulated within an economic/competitive framework fail to meet the needs of many students and teachers and calls for a new paradigm for policy development, one that emphasizes the relationships between "education and democratic humanism" (p. 33).

In the same vein, Bellah and colleagues (1985) note that an ethic of competition is concerned with the ability to outperform others. Thus, it has an individualistic emphasis, for competition, by its very nature, separates individuals and groups. These authors believe that educational values and practices have been greatly influenced by our culture's simultaneous commitments to individualism and to success understood as winning in some arena. Indeed, they state that educational practices, in addition to being affected by these values, have also been instrumental in perpetuating them. Citing the work of Eva Brann (1979), they write that "in education at present . . . technique has become far too dominant" (p. 203). This dominance both reflects and creates a belief that "education [is] an instrument for individual careerism" (p. 293), a view consistent with a competitive ethic that would emphasize the morality of actions that increase one's chances to succeed.

Shortcomings of an Economic Model and a Competitive Ethic

With Bellah and his co-authors, I contend that an economic model, with its competitive emphasis, falls short of being an adequate perspective for concerned administrators because it fails to deal satisfactorily with two critical issues. First, this model only superficially addresses questions regarding values. It thus fails to provide guidance for educational leaders whose work inevitably requires that they make value judgments (Giroux, 1988a; Greenfield, 1991; Hodgkinson, 1978, 1983, 1991; Purpel, 1989; Sergiovanni, 1980, 1984, 1987; Starratt, 1991). Second, an economic-competitive model is predicated on the assumption that goals and methods that, in some instances, have worked in business settings are appropriate and workable in education. Such an assumption lacks support in both logic and evidence (see Callahan, 1962; Murphy, 1991).

In his discussion of the inability of economic conceptions to address educational values, Giroux (1988a) expresses concern over "the gathering momentum of the current reform period to redefine the purpose of education so as to eliminate its citizenship function in favor of a narrowly defined labor market perspective" (p. 17). This trend, in his view, drastically undermines education because it fails to acknowledge the importance of schools' promoting "equality, liberty, and human life [values] at the center of notions of democracy and citizenship" (p. 28). Finkelstein (1984) agrees and argues that, when an economic perspective dominates the thinking of educators and policy makers, they can "forge no new visions of political and social possibilities" (p. 280). Similarly, Purpel (1989) claims that the tendency to allow economic concerns and strategies to overshadow distinctively educational ones has resulted in moral impotence in school settings.

> Our consciousness has reverted and regressed to one involving scarcity, survival, competition, and stagnation. The language of growth, potential, daring, and challenge has become muted: a sense of infinite possibility has been replaced by timidity, expansiveness of caution, long-range thinking by the bottom line, visions by quotas. (p. 15)

In addition to the fact that it thwarts discussions of important educational values, an economic-competitive model of schools has another weakness. Its assumption that schools are analogous to profit-driven businesses and that strategies intended to improve the latter translate easily into the former is theoretically and empirically suspect. In regard to analogies between schools and businesses, Hodgkinson (1991) suggests that education's purposes are "special" and unique. For this reason, he contends that any attempt to equate schools with other organizations and to automatically transfer principles, strategies, and ethical commitments from the latter to the former is logically untenable.

The problems that arise in applying economic models to schools are not merely conceptual in nature. Several scholars suggest that many practical strategies emerging from the belief that what works in the marketplace will work in schools have failed (or will fail) to live up to their promises. For example, the belief that competition between students, teachers, administrators, or schools can and will produce excellence is both conceptually and empirically suspect. It is grounded in "the a priori assumption that the virtues of competition in the marketplace can be made applicable to any organizational endeavor, including the education of our children" (Evans, 1990, p. 12). Offering persuasive arguments refuting this assumption, Evans notes that the idea "that a cause and effect relationship exists between competition and quality in the marketplace and that a similar dynamic would work with schools" (p. 12) is based on several questionable beliefs. These include such ideas as: "competition leads to quality;

. . . corporate America knows best; . . . parents [consumers] will make wise choices . . . [and] lay decision makers are superior to [educational] professionals" (p. 12).

Evidence from a number of studies supports Evans's perspective and suggests that excessive competition actually may have an adverse effect on achievement. The concept of career ladders, predicated on the belief that teaching improves as educators battle for status and merit pay, has come under fire from several fronts. Sergiovanni and Starratt (1988) cite a study by Lovell and Phelps (1976) that suggests that "the plan [the Tennessee career ladder] has resulted in a number of unanticipated and negative consequences—consequences which could be interpreted as decreasing the quality of work life in teaching, the quality of teaching and learning, and the attractiveness of the profession" (p. 24). Schlechty (1989), even while advocating "the *concept* of career ladder" (p. 357) because of its link to teacher professionalization and increased "career earning power" (p. 356), notes that

> In action, many career ladder programs have tended to become bureaucratic and stifling. Rather than encouraging good teachers to remain in teaching, they have prompted good teachers to leave the classroom. Rather than motivating all teachers, they have rewarded a few and inherently punished many. (p. 356)

Evidence also suggests that competition between students may not be the best technique for encouraging achievement. Aljose and Joyner (1990) and Johnson and Johnson (1989) review a number of studies that suggest that competitive learning strategies are generally related to lower levels of mastery than are cooperative ones.

> Over 185 studies have compared the impact of cooperation and competitive situations on achievement. The results of these studies indicated that cooperation promoted higher individual achievement and greater group productivity than did competition (effect size = 0.67). When studies were rated according to their methodological rigor and only the high quality studies were included in the analyses, the results were considerably stronger (effect size = 0.88). (Johnson & Johnson, 1989, p. 170)

The competition advocated by many has been not merely the type that takes place between individuals or groups. In recent years unquestioning acceptance of an economic model has given rise to calls for stiffer standards in all educational arenas. Many calling for higher standards to encourage educational excellence seem to assume that these standards should be set a bit higher than current norms and high enough to ensure that our students achieve more than students in other countries. Those taking this perspective fail to reckon with the passive role this forces on American educators. In essence, the standards being proposed are quite relative and could go up or down depending on a number of factors. Further, quite often the standards are set *outside* of schools—by government agencies or task forces, by representatives of the corporate world, or others. If, for example, mean scores on a norm-referenced test declined between 1991 and 1995, high 1995 standards could actually be lower than those of 1991. And if, for some reason, the achievement level of students in Japan or Germany declined, then standards for U.S. students could be lowered without destroying a competitive edge. The standard advocated by a caring ethic is based on something far more stable than norms for any given group or year.

Caring's Response to the Performance Challenge

An economic model of schools and a competitive ethic accept uncritically the idea that education can and should be valued in quantifiable terms, terms set by the marketplace or some other force outside of education. A caring ethic and the model of schooling it assumes and promotes provide a different perspective on this topic. Foundational to caring is a belief in the intrinsic value of persons (Noddings, 1984; Starratt, 1991). In affirming this, it defines enterprises as ethical to the extent that they promote human development, welfare, and happiness. Grounded in this ontological, unconditional conception of value, this perspective emphasizes that students, teachers, and administrators deserve a supportive, nurturing educational environment—*simply because they are persons.* If accepted, this view would clearly influence administrative scholarship, policy, and action. The burning question for school leaders would become, "Does this act or decision have the potential to positively affect personal development?" rather than "What are the likely monetary outcomes of this decision?"

This is a good place to note that a caring ethic does not negate the importance of academic achievement, vocational competence, or economic health, for these contribute to both personal and community well-being (Higgins, 1989; Hobbs et al., 1984; Mitchell, 1990a, 1990b; Perkins, 1976, 1982). The values of caring actually subsume those held by leaders accepting a competitive ethic. The latter would consider the achievement of dominance in the marketplace to be chief reason for education. The former, on the other hand, emphasizing the worth of persons, would view anything that promoted personal development—including academic and vocational competency—as being of value.

In addition to offering an expanded conception of educational values and purposes, a caring ethic offers an expanded perspective on pedagogical and administrative strategies. As noted above, the standards raising movement has received much attention in recent years. I argue that standards embraced by an ethic of care are actually higher than those set by government agencies, standardized test scores, or GNPs of other countries. They would be not unlike the standards a loving parent might set for a child. Such a mother or father would want full development, great happiness, and optimum mental, emotional, and relational health for her or his child. Further, this parent would desire a healthy community and world in which the child could grow. A caring educational ethic would support the idea that schools should promote maximum individual and community growth and development and not settle for simply achieving more—on some set of indicators—than others. Significantly, this represents a standard unlikely to change quickly or easily. This could be quite important if education began to produce students with competencies beyond (or different from) those needed by the labor force, for under these conditions market-driven standards conceivably might work against optimum intellectual achievement. (See Martin, 1990, and Shea, 1990, for a more complete discussion of this possibility.)

In terms of pedagogy, cooperative learning strategies that, according to research, have had impressive effects on learning (e.g., Aljose & Joyner, 1990) are certainly consistent with an ethic of care. Johnson and Johnson (1989), for example, note the links between this ethic, pedagogical techniques promoting interdependence, and achievement.

> Joint efforts to achieve tend to create caring and committed relationships. Caring comes, not from memos and announcements, but from the bonding that results from joint efforts. Correspondingly, long-term persistent, committed efforts do not come from the head, they come from the heart. Achievement is powered by caring and committed personal relationships (not tangible rewards or intellectual rationales). (p. 168)

Case studies by Dillon (1989), Grant (1988), Lightfoot (1983), and Maeroff (1990) similarly suggest a link between noncompetitive classrooms, a nurturing school climate, caring administrators, and students' academic achievement.

Ashton and Webb (1986) note relationships between teachers' sense of efficacy, positive interpersonal relationships with students, and student academic achievement. These scholars do not specifically credit caring relationships as a first cause in this three-way linkage, and, indeed, the concept of causation in complex human interactions is problematic in most circumstances. Others do, however, emphasize that teachers' feeling cared for and being able to nurture students are foundational to vocational satisfaction (Chase-Lansdale, Dempsey, Noblitt, & Rogers, 1991; Louis, 1990). Lightfoot (1983), Sergiovanni (1989), and Starratt (1991) specifically emphasize the link between caring administrators and teachers' sense of efficacy, happiness, and commitment.

CHALLENGE TWO: BATTLING SOCIAL PROBLEMS

Influence of a Legal/Judicial Model

The chorus of voices calling on schools to attend to students' mastery of academic and technical skills in order to ensure an educated workforce is certainly not the only one clamoring for attention. Another large group of reformers, aware of changes in the fabric of society, look to educators to take a leading role in battling a number of social problems (Beck & Murphy, 1993; Carnegie Council on Adolescent Development, 1989). These problems range from inequities due to poverty, race, and gender, to school or district level concerns such as gangs, vandalism, truancy, adolescent suicide, teen pregnancy, and the like. Discussions of these concerns frequently presuppose a legal or judicial model of schools. That is, they call on educators to define their roles and responsibilities ever mindful of legislative mandates and constraints that might guide or restrict their activities.

The complexity and diversity of problems—framed within this model—pose dilemmas for administrators. Leaders sensitive to student needs and to demands coming from adults within and outside of schools could find themselves devoting large portions of time and energy to nonacademic concerns and, concomitantly, paying less attention to schools' academic mission. In so doing, they risk criticism for failing to meet the expectations of many taxpayers and policy makers who feel that educators are not being paid to engage in "social work." State and local administrators also must make difficult decisions about just and equitable distributions of opportunities and resources; they must seek to address the complex challenges of educating a diverse population; and, frequently, they must stretch fewer dollars over expanding programs and student bodies. Furthermore, they must formulate responses to calls from physicians, government officials, and professional educators who propose that school leaders make AIDS education a top priority (e.g., Centers for Disease Control, 1988; Council for Chief State School Offices, 1988; National School Board Association, 1987; *Report of the Surgeon General's Workshop on Children with HIV Infection*, 1986; United States Department of Education, 1987; Weinstein, 1989). Additionally, they must determine the school's role in responding to teens' need for contraceptive education and for support if pregnancy occurs (e.g., Compton, Duncan, & Hruska, 1987; Pilat, 1991; Vinovskis, 1988). Schools, further, have been cited as appropriate fronts to wage war on drug use and abuse and other forms of juvenile crime (e.g., Erdberg, 1988; Golubchick, 1989). And school leaders are expected to offer programs to assist recovering addicts and victims of sexual and physical abuse (e.g., Beck & Marshall, 1992; Elshtain, 1988). Indeed, a large number of scholars seem to consider the amelioration of social problems as a central mission of schools (e.g., Bane, 1989; Brofenbrenner, 1988; Elkind, 1981, 1984, 1987; Gilligan, 1982; Noddings, 1984).

The challenge to address these problems actually forces school leaders to grapple with a number of questions. For below the surface of concerns raised by these issues lie questions regarding the legal and ethical purpose(s) of schools and the meaning of concepts such as morality, responsibility, equity, and justice. Furthermore, responsive leaders must seek ways to achieve an appropriate balance between the often conflicting values of quality and equality (Hobbs et al., 1984; Marshall, Mitchell, & Wirt, 1989). They must also contend with the possibility of criticism and, in extreme cases, lawsuits because of their decisions (Chilman, 1983; Paul & Pilpel, 1979; Pilpel & Rockett, 1981; Scales, 1983).

These diverse demands and administrative responses to them assume that justice, equity, and the right to "life, liberty, and the pursuit of happiness," values at the heart of a democratic legal system, are primary educational values and that the chief mission of schools is to institutionalize and maintain these values. They also assume that schools are key places to correct problems related to these issues. Furthermore, those analyzing schools within this model place great faith in policy as a force capable of ensuring that these values are protected.

A Utilitarian Ethic and a Legal/Judicial Model

Many ethical perspectives certainly influence the thinking of persons operating within this framework. A common thread does, however, run through all of them. Those who focus on battling social problems in schools are concerned with developing a functional educational system that supports a democratic society. In other words, they are motivated by an instrumental or utilitarian ethic, as described by Frankena (1973).

> There are less precise ways of defining utilitarianism, which I shall use for convenience, but in my use of the term I shall mean the view that the ultimate standard of right, wrong, and obligation is the principle of utility which says quite strictly that the moral end to be sought in all we do is the greatest possible balance of good over evil (or the least possible balance of evil over good) in the world as a whole. Here "good" and "evil" mean nonmoral good and evil. (pp. 34–35)

These words describe the perspective that, in many ways, drives the thinking of those who believe schools and their leaders should focus on promoting—in the larger society—"the greatest possible balance of good over evil."

Campbell and co-authors, in their seminal *A History of Thought and Practice in Educational Administration* (1987), discuss the ascendence of this ethical perspective. They note that beginning in the late 1940s an increasingly heterogeneous student population pushed administrators into addressing a range of social issues that they had previously been able to avoid. This occurred at a time when several forces—the wave of patriotism following World War II, the rise of the human relations movement in business and industry, and a growing belief that schools should be run on the basis of rational, nonvalue-oriented principles—were exercising much influence on the thought and practice of school leaders. In the spirit of postwar America, educators began to embrace the concept that schools must, first and foremost, be "institutions in which . . . democratic beliefs and attitudes" (p. 59) are perpetuated and "the spirit of American life [is] . . . maintained" (p. 59). And, lest they appear to be yielding to nonrational values, school leaders looked to laws and policies emanating from legislatures and courtrooms, for these, ostensibly, had been derived by an objective examination of the facts. This, it seems, offered a "safe" and useful approach to administrators and satisfied proponents of the three forces noted above.

During the past three decades, the conception of the school's role in battling social issues has expanded. Campbell and co-authors (1987), for example, note that "Great Society programs" (p. 83) took the battle against poverty into schools. Focusing on another problem, Vinovskis (1988) tells of the ways the Carter administration's concern over teenage pregnancy prompted a host of educational policies and programs. Brad Mitchell (1990a), citing Cohen (1976), suggests that our culture has changed at a breakneck pace, resulting in "numerous forms of loss" (p. 31) in virtually every area of life. He underscores the fact that this loss has, in recent years, prompted a range of educational policies. "Cohen was right; a national sense of loss and social policy for public education have formed a double helix bond in the sociohistorical development of modern America" (p. 31). As noted earlier in this section, the past decade has witnessed the growth of the assumption that schools are the best place to fight youthful drug use, to stop the spread of AIDS among teens, to help young people make wise sexuality decisions, and to offer counseling and remediation to students with physical or psychological problems. Those promoting this assumption use many points in this discussion. Most, however, do ground their arguments in the belief that public schools—because they are public—are legally appropriate arenas to attack social problems (Cohen, 1976; Mitchell, 1990b). Furthermore, most scholars calling for specific policies and programs draw justification for their plans from a utilitarian ethic. Their emphasis tends to be on the likelihood that what they propose will indeed work in ameliorating some problems.

Shortcomings of a Legal/Judicial Model and a Utilitarian Ethic

A legal/judicial model with its stress on a utilitarian ethic, however, has proven unsatisfactory as the dominant framework to guide educational administrators. Several shortcomings are especially noteworthy. First, this perspective is reductionistic and diminishes the personal/human dimensions of education. Second, it fails to distinguish adequately between means and ends. Third, this framework has a short-term focus, virtually ignoring the reality that a complex set of forces, often deeply embedded in our culture, influences the development of social problems and that responding to these requires that administrators understand this complexity and recognize that short-term solutions are of value only if they contribute to more lasting improvement. Finally, this view is naively optimistic in its assumption that rational educational policies and programs can solve complex social problems.

The first shortcoming results from the fact that a legal/judicial/utilitarian model takes a rather impersonal view of schools and of those who inhabit them, focusing on "the general" or "nonmoral good" (Frankena, 1973, pp. 34, 35) and "avoid[ing] encroaching on individuals' private concerns" (Strike, 1982, p. 92). In this regard, Oliver (1976) asserts that socially oriented reforms, grounded in legislative or judicial mandates, assume that education must focus on "improving the quality of collective primary group life" and pay little attention to "the promotion of individual growth" (p. 14). He further claims that this perspective emphasizes the promotion of "a single, cohesive society" (Oliver, 1976, p. 9) and deemphasizes individuals, "subcultures," and "subsocieties" (p. 9).

A second weakness of this model lies in its tendency to concentrate on means and ignore the educational ends those means are intended to achieve. In her discussion of policy options to improve urban schools, Michelle Fine (1992) warns against this tendency. She suggests that many educational reformers, grappling with the rights of various stakeholders while simultaneously seeking solutions to problems of overcrowded, at times dangerous, or ineffective schools, tend to gravitate toward short-term, quick-fix strategies, which improve opportunities for "a small and creamy slice of teachers and students protected from bureaucracy . . . [or] a privileged slice of private/parochial schools which will profit from vouchers" (p. 32) and have lost sight of legitimate ends of public education in a democratic society—"intellectual growth and personal development" (p. 29) for *all*. Recognizing that holding to this ultimate goal is difficult, Fine nevertheless asserts that it is the only option for educators committed to caring, justice, and the public good.

Bellah and his co-authors (1985) also caution against overlooking the ultimate ends or purposes of education. Indeed, they argue that social movements designed to "eliminate overt expressions of discrimination" and, by extension, of any other social problem that do not have as their ultimate goal "personal transformation among large numbers" (p. 286) may actually exacerbate some problems they seek to eliminate.

Another characteristic of an instrumental-utilitarian ethic that poses potential problems for school leaders is its tendency to focus on proximal rather than distal causes of problems and effects of solutions. (See Scarr, 1985, for a discussion of this tendency in a number of social science disciplines.) The recent history of educational administration reveals that this short-term emphasis has, indeed, influenced the schooling enterprise. In the past four decades, leaders have swung back and forth on issues, including tracking (Oakes, 1985), vocational education (Adler, 1982; Goodlad, 1984), sexuality education programs (Chilman, 1983; Vinovskis, 1988), teacher and pupil evaluation strategies (Darling-Hammond, 1985; LeShan, 1985; Schlechty, 1989), the usefulness of empirical data in guiding planning (Campbell et al., 1987), plans for organizing the school day (Noddings, 1988; Sergiovanni, 1987), governance structures (Bacharach & Conley, 1989; Clark & Meloy, 1989; Ferguson, 1984), and the roles of superintendents and principals (Beck & Murphy, 1993; Cuban, 1976; Tyack & Hansot, 1982). These swings seem to have had some negative effects. Administrators admit to "role conflict" (Dodd, 1965, p. 1-1) due to conflicting expectations. Teachers feel frustrated, and many leave the profession (Ashton & Webb, 1986; Lortie, 1975; Rosenholtz & Simpson, 1990; Sizer, 1985); students experience a loss of continuity (Cohen, 1976; Elkind, 1981; Mitchell, 1990a; Oliver, 1976) and of a sense of membership in a community (Bellah et al., 1985; Keniston, 1965; Oliver, 1976).

A final problem with a legal/judicial model of schooling is its naive faith that policies and programs designed to remedy some social problem really can transform either schools or society. A number of scholars, including Bates (1983), Bellah and co-authors (1985), Fay (1975), Foster (1986b), Noddings (1984), Oliver (1976), Purpel (1989), Sergiovanni (1989), and Starratt (1991), discuss this inadequacy. Oliver (1976), for example, argues that "the devout utilitarian [who assumes that] the road to progress is straightforward and consists of making schooling more efficient and effective [via mandates and top-down directives]" (p. 37) looks at "only one part of the human condition" and ignores emotional needs such as the need for secure interpersonal relationships. Sergiovanni (1989) contrasts *"policy as stated* and *policy in use"* (p. 4). The former, in his view, is of limited effectiveness in solving educational problems. The latter, on the other hand, represents solutions that are developed by "principals, teachers, and students as schooling takes place" (p. 4) and that have the potential for success in effecting positive changes. (See also Lipsky, 1969, and Crowson & Porter-Gehrie, 1980.) Beck and Marshall's (1992) research on efforts to solve problems related to adolescent sexuality revealed similar results. They found that educators seeking to deal with teens on sensitive issues were driven by their commitment to young people and guided by instincts, experience, professional training, and situational demands—not by policy mandates or guidelines.

Caring's Contribution to Battling Social Problems

A caring ethic addresses each of these weaknesses and provides a broader, more comprehensive platform to guide administrative thought and practice. As noted earlier, caring is distinguished by its steadfast commitment to promoting total development, a commitment that necessitates working for both individual and community health. This conception of purpose is different from that which drives a utilitarian ethic. The latter and its related model assume that, in the event of a conflict between individual and corporate well-being, action that brings the best outcome for the entire social organism should prevail. In contrast, a caring ethic assumes that such a conflict, if it exists, is superficial and that a deeper examination of the situation will reveal that personal, private concerns and the public good are linked and that solutions to problems must seek to promote both. Indeed, it would argue that administrators who fail to do this and seek to solve social problems at the expense of persons are rather like the stereotypical surgeon who describes an operation as a success even if the patient dies.

Additionally, a caring ethic claims that the establishment of smoothly functioning, democratic schools where justice, fairness, and the like are upheld is not the end of administrative activity. Instead, it views these as means toward the end of promoting the total development of each student and teacher, of the various communities affected by the organization, and, ultimately, of society at large.

Indeed, central to a caring ethic are an emphasis on the intrinsic value of human beings and a belief that actions motivated by this ethic will be characterized by an unconditional commitment to persons. Educators adhering to this ethic will find themselves in agreement with Sergiovanni (1987), Starratt (1991), Buber (1965), Gilligan (1982), and Noddings (1984) that education is a human enterprise and that its finest purpose is promoting the fullest growth and development of persons. In so doing, they will assert that "the integrity of human relationships should be held sacred and that the school as an organization should hold the good of human beings within it as sacred" (Starratt, 1991, p. 195). Caring leaders will surely seek ways to remedy social problems, but the value of these remedies will be relative to the "absolute value of human persons-in-relationship." A caring ethic—with its enduring commitment to persons, its concern with the continued ecological health of schools and their related communities, and its view that human needs must not be ignored—has the potential to ground and focus administrative thought and to protect educators from being swayed by quick-fix, short-term solutions to complex problems.

Finally, an ethic of care holds that persons must go beyond the letter of the law in their attempts to address social problems. While not derogating the importance of policies and mandates, educators guided by caring seek to interact with others as colleagues, co-learners, and friends. Describing schools that "have gone beyond isolated elements of remedial actions and made more comprehensive changes" (p. 225), Lisbeth Schorr (1989) notes that, within these institutions, "respectful, trusting personal relationships among children, teachers, principal, and parents" (pp. 241–242) are present. She further asserts that these caring interactions are as central to schools' effectiveness as adherence to formal plans, policies, or sets of guidelines (or perhaps more so). Her words suggest that, when addressing social problems, leaders guided by caring would place the needs, concerns, and beliefs of those they lead above the dictates or mandates of some policy-making body. For them, rules and guidelines would represent only the minimum acceptable response to another. Those who cared would seek, consistently, to go beyond this minimum.

CHALLENGE THREE: RETHINKING ORGANIZATIONAL STRATEGIES

Influence of a Political Model

A third challenge to theorists and practitioners comes from persons and groups who call for major changes in school governance structures. The traditional bureaucratic model, with its focus on centralized authority, clear chains of command, defined roles, and the rational pursuit of quantifiable goals, has come under attack from many quarters (for an overview, see Beck & Murphy, 1993; Murphy, 1991). Two dimensions of this challenge have especially attracted attention. For many, the chief issue is the development of structures capable of dealing with the complexity of educating a diverse population in a postindustrial world (Maccoby, 1988). For others, reconceptualization of leadership in restructured schools is a central concern (Beck & Murphy, 1993; Sergiovanni, 1987). When writing about these issues, authors seem to view schools as "'alive and screaming' political arenas that house a complex variety of individual and group interests" (Bolman & Deal, 1991, p. 186). They concentrate on the rights, interests, and powers of various stakeholders and, depending on their perspective, recommend certain new structures and suggest strategies by which these might be attained.

Several themes tend to recur in the writings of those calling for reconstruction of educational structures. First, most agree that a bureaucratic, top-down model is no longer appropriate, effective, or efficient. Murphy (1990c) argues that this belief was, in fact, the dominant concern of Wave 2 (1986–1989) reformers, including Boyd (1987), Chubb (1988), Cuban (1984), Elmore (1988), Sedlack and co-authors (1986), and Sizer (1985). Differing somewhat in their proposed solutions, these scholars agree that traditional structures are inadequate for supporting educational efforts into the next century. For the most part, their concerns are functional in nature. Others, however, attack bureaucracies from an ideological perspective. Ferguson (1984), for example, argues that traditional structures are oppressive especially to women, to racial minorities, and to the poor. In the same vein, Clark and Meloy (1989) "renounc[e] bureaucracy" (p. 272) in educational structures. Primarily concerned with the negative effects of such a system on teachers, they call for "the development of and experimentation with new organizational forms" (p. 293), forms that stress democratic process, shared decision making, and the like. Wise (1989) and Bacharach and Conley (1989) note that bureaucratically organized schools are becoming increasingly anachronistic as teacher professionalization becomes a widely accepted concept. Kirst (1989), in turn, discusses the failure of governance systems that vest power chiefly in state level agencies and positions.

Virtually all who criticize bureaucracies offer suggestions for alternative organizational structures. Murphy (1991) notes that recommended systems tend to be decentralized (Guthrie, 1990; Murphy & Hart, 1988) and more professionally controlled (David, 1989; Houston, 1989). Furthermore, they usually are pictured as exhibiting the following features: alterations in traditional relationship patterns (Conley, 1989; Rallis, 1990); lateral rather than vertical authority flows (Clark & Meloy, 1989); flexible role definitions (Corcoran, 1989); leadership based on competence rather than position (American Association of Colleges of Teacher Education, 1988; Angus, 1988); and independence and isolation replaced by cooperative work (Beare, 1989).

A chief concern of those who write of these new organizational forms is empowerment—of principals, of teachers, of parents, and even of students (see, e.g., Carnegie Forum on Education and the Economy, 1986; Chubb, 1988; Giroux, 1988a, 1988b; Giroux & McLaren, 1988; Holmes Group, 1986; Kearnes, 1988a, 1988b; Murphy, 1990a; Sergiovanni, 1989). In some instances, the concept of choice, especially parental choice, is linked with empowerment; in others, it relates to redistributions of power and to changes in the school's authority structures. Regardless of these nuances, the concept of empowerment has been central in the thinking of those calling for new organizational structures.

The Influence of a "Liberationist" Ethic

Many, viewing schools within this political model, suggest that a dominant administrative ethic should be one that seeks a redistribution of power and resources, taking from those who have more and giving to those who have less. Several terms have been used in discussions of this ethic. Rudder (1991) describes ethical principles concerned with "public moral issues" as "political" (p. 75). Frankena (1973) suggests that utilitarianism and justice often have great relevance for issues related to the distribution of power and resources. Cusick (1983) refers to the "egalitarian ideal" (p. 1) as the guiding value for administrative actions seeking "social, political, and economic equality" (p. 1), and Strike (1982) suggests that "liberal views of social justice" (p. 1) influence the ethics of school leaders concerned with the political dimensions of education. In an effort to capture the emphases of these various scholars, I have coined the term "liberationist" to describe the the ethic that influences many of the calls for changes in educational governance. A liberationist ethic is one that "posits as fundamental that men subjected to domination must fight for emancipation" (Freire, 1970, p. 74, quoted in Dokecki, 1982, p. 194). When applied to school governance, this ethic would consider actions moral to the extent that they promote radical redistributions of power, leading to victory for oppressed classes in the fight for emancipation.

Shortcomings of a "Liberationist" Ethic and a Political Model

As a dominant principle, this radical ethic, like those stressing competition and utility, is inadequate as a guide for school leaders and needs perspectives offered by caring as a complement, guard, and guide. Three aspects of a liberationist ethic are especially problematic for educators. First, this perspective has an incomplete view of power and, thus, is of limited usefulness to educators. Second, this ethic, because of its emphasis on the overthrow of existing structures, is likely to be more rhetorical than practical in actually effecting organizational change. Finally, a liberationist ethic is useful only in certain situations. It has little to say about the conduct of the many interactions in the day-to-day life of schools. Within a political framework, power is viewed as a limited "scarce resource" (Kanter, 1977, p. 195) found in greater abundance at higher organizational levels. It is frequently linked with formal roles and is considered to be what enables some to exercise "authority and domination" (Dunlap & Goldman, 1991, p. 7) over others. Those who call for structures that redistribute this resource tend to stress the moral legitimacy and importance of taking power from those who traditionally have possessed it and, in some way, giving it to those who have not. In the reform vernacular of the last decade, this process, as noted earlier, is most often discussed in terms of "empowerment" (e.g., Foster, 1986a; Sergiovanni, 1989; Shulman, 1989; Thomas, 1990).

This concept of power fails to capture several important dimensions of influence patterns in educational settings. For example, it fails to recognize that, in education, power is not a limited resource that must be subtracted and added in some fashion. Rather, it is a phenomenon, which can and should be exponentially increased by the educative process. Dunlap and Goldman (1991) offer helpful insights into the unique nature of power in schools. They argue that "traditional definitions of power" (p. 7), as offered by Abbott and Caracheo (1988), Etzioni (1960), French and Raven (1959), Hobbes (1839), Machiavelli (1952, originally published 1532), Thompson (1956), Weber (1947), and others, leave scholars with a "black hole of non-explanation . . . [about] how acts of power could and do occur in education" (p. 13). Implicit in their discussion is the notion that, insofar as traditional conceptions dominate the thinking of educators, they mislead and misdirect efforts to empower all persons in school settings.

For educators who genuinely desire to see changes in governance systems, a liberationist ethic, as a dominant perspective, poses another problem. It tends to emphasize the overthrow of existing structures and to stress the moral rightness of any actions leading to this overthrow. Such a view is likely to have more of a rhetorical, than an actual, impact. To be sure, the inflammatory language of the calls for radical organizational structures has a place in educational scholarship. It expresses moral outrage over injustice and oppression and points to the fact that alternatives to the status quo do exist (Foster, 1986a; Giroux, Penna, & Pinar, 1981; Purpel, 1989; Starratt, 1991). Such a view is not, however, likely to lead to constructive or creative dialogues with those currently in power. Indeed, such a vigorous advocate of emancipatory structures as Henry Giroux (1988a) argues that discourses and dialogues most likely to effect genuine change "should not be based exclusively on a language of critique, one that, for instance, limits its focus on the schools to the elimination of relations of subordination and inequality" (p. 31).

A final problem with a liberationist ethic as a dominant administrative guide is its limited applicability. It offers a perspective on moral actions in situations where structural oppression exists. It says little about the day-to-day conduct of life during or after a change process. Because it does not deal with routine concerns, this ethic must be complemented or supplemented by others, for moral philosophy must go beyond solving problems and inform daily events and interactions (Hauerwas, 1983).

Caring's Perspective on Structural and Organizational Challenges

Radical ethics and change strategies undoubtedly have a place in education. They need, however, the grounding offered by an ecologically oriented ethic of care. For, in caring, one can find a sound and useful conception of educational power, a language that promises to facilitate dialogue between various interest groups, and a perspective capable of providing sustained guidance for persons within schools that have restructured or reorganized successfully.

In their critique of traditional understandings of power, Dunlap and Goldman (1991) describe a type that, in their view, is appropriate for educational settings. They offer the term "facilitative power" (p. 13) in an effort to capture the reality of "individual and collective agency within school structures" (p. 13) and note:

> Facilitative power reflects a process that, by creating or sustaining favorable conditions, allows subordinates to enhance their individual and collective performance. If dominance is power *over* someone, facilitative power is power

manifested through someone more like Clegg's (1981) images of electrical or
ecological circuits of power than like the ability to break or smash something
by force. (p. 13)

Administrators seeking to exercise this type of power find, in caring, a useful and appropriate ethical perspective, for caring's emphasis on cooperation
and supportive interactions is central to the concept of facilitation. Indeed,
Dunlap and Goldman's statement about facilitative power's enhancing of "individual *and* collective performance . . . [and its working through] ecological
circuits" (p. 13, emphasis added) coincides with caring's refusal to separate
persons and their communities and its concomitant intention to seek the development of both. These authors also emphasize that "facilitative power [will]
contribut[e] to a cumulative reduction in administrators' formal authority, [and]
it will also likely reduce the degree to which they are at the visible center of
schools" (p. 25). Again, this idea is consistent with caring's emphasis on service
and other-centered activities. Administrators who think of their power in terms
of facilitation and service would support and actively work toward nonbureaucratic structures, "increasing the capacity of others . . . and . . . minimizing controlling acts" (p. 23). These structures would emphasize the "professional autonomy" (p. 24) of teachers, the value of collaborative pedagogical and
management strategies, and honest communication among all persons in school
systems (see also Greenleaf, 1977).

In addition to offering an alternative conceptualization of power, a caring
ethic emphasizes an idea that, at least ostensibly, is agreed upon by government
officials, practicing educators, mainstream scholars and researchers, critical theorists, radical feminists, and a host of other educational stakeholders. This is
the belief that education should promote—not hinder—the "quality of life"
(Starratt, 1991, p. 200). In his "Building an Ethical School: A Theory for Practice in Educational Leadership" (1991), Starratt emphasizes that an ethic of
care, when joined with ethics of justice and critique, can promote "open, trusting, professional communication" (p. 195). In the absence of caring, other ethics
run the risk of encouraging "mistrust, manipulation, aggressive and controlling
actions or language . . . [that] can lead to a relationship that is hypocritical, dis-
honest, disloyal, vicious, and dehumanizing" (p. 200). These negative relationships are unlikely to result in the establishment of effective organizational structures. Caring relationships have the potential to provide a foundation on which
such structures can be built.

Finally, caring offers a perspective necessary to and capable of guiding day-
to-day activities and interactions within schools. Unlike competitive and liberationist ethics that assume that life is a series of struggles in which persons or
organizations are, in some way, pitted against each other, caring assumes that
individuals are interrelated and interdependent and so life is, fundamentally, a

process of mutual growth. Insofar as day-to-day educational activities are (or should be) aimed at enhancing this development, an ethic of care holds promise for enhancing the lives of principals, teachers, and students.

SUMMARY

Starratt (1991) argues that the ethical practice of educational administration demands "a multidimensional construct that offers practicing administrators a way to think about their work and workplace" (p. 186). He recommends "the joining of three ethics: the ethic of critique, the ethic of justice, and the ethic of caring" (p. 186). My assessment of the ethical perspective needed to meet administrative challenges agrees with that of Starratt, with one exception. He pictures critique, justice, and caring as equally important guides to moral action. I, in contrast, place caring at the top of the values hierarchy. I propose that a number of ethics have a place in educational leadership but that each needs to be informed and guided by caring. By emphasizing the absolute value of each person and the moral and practical necessity to act in ways that support both individuals and their societies, caring reminds us that the ends promoted by competitive, utilitarian, and liberationist ethics find their value in their ability to promote personal and community well-being.

5 The Caring Practitioner

If we desire a relevant science of administration, then the worlds
of descriptive, normative, and interpretive science must be
brought together to bear on the problem of professional practice.
(Thomas Sergiovanni, 1984, "Developing a Relevant Theory
of Administration," in T. J. Sergiovanni and J. E. Corbally (Eds.),
Leadership and Organizational Culture, p. 290)

Let us not love with words or tongue but with actions and in truth.
(I John 4:6)

Thus far, I have focused on establishing a conceptual framework for understanding the place of a caring ethic in educational administration. In this chapter, I examine ways this ethic can and should affect administrative practice. In
order to do this, I discuss three role labels that could be used to describe a
caring educational leader: (1) values-driven organizer; (2) capable and creative
pedagogue; and (3) cultivator of a nurturing culture. These labels emphasize
three central administrative tasks: organizing structures and systems, leading in
the instructional arena, and promoting a distinct and healthy school culture.
The tone of this discussion is, by design, reflective rather than prescriptive.
Drawing insights and examples from theorists, researchers, and practitioners, I
offer these ideas in the hope that they might provide a kind of jump start for
school leaders desiring to operate under an ethic of care. To facilitate clear
discussion, I approach these as if they are discrete phenomena. In reality, they
are not; decisions and actions in any arena have very real effects on the others.
Caring leaders would recognize these linkages. Indeed, this ethic provides a
perspective capable of tying administrative tasks to the promotion of personal
and community development.

THE CARING ADMINISTRATOR AS A VALUES-DRIVEN ORGANIZER

Traditionally, educational administrators have made decisions according to
the tenets of "pyramidal (bureaucratic) management models" (Guthrie, 1990,
p. 214). Influenced by Blau and Scott (1962), Fayol (1949, originally published
1919), Perrow (1986), Taylor (1911), Weber (1947), and by models from busi-

ness and industry, superintendents and principals have looked to rationally established goals to guide them in their organizational strategies (Campbell et al., 1987). They have, thus, attempted to "coordinat[e] and control" (Bolman & Deal, 1991, p. 24; see also Guthrie, 1990) events and persons by developing "rules, policies, standard operating procedures, information systems . . . or a variety of more informal techniques" (Bolman & Deal, 1991, p. 48) in order to accomplish these goals.

A caring ethic would lead administrators to look beyond goals to several distinctive values to guide them in developing organizational strategies. They would embrace the idea that each person deserves the opportunity to live and learn in a supportive, nurturing environment. Goal-setting and organizational strategies would occur under this fundamental assumption. Caring school leaders would hold in their minds an image of institutions where all—students, teachers, and administrators—flourish. Furthermore, they would perceive the links between the health of schools and their inhabitants and that of the larger society. They would, thus, seek structures, systems, and methods capable of promoting personal and community well-being. This process would, in all likelihood, involve undertaking three tasks. Administrators would:

1. Thoughtfully and reflectively cultivate a "driving vision [that would imbue] decisions and practices with meaning, placing powerful emphasis on why things are done as well as how" (Lipsitz, 1984, quoted in Sergiovanni, 1987, p. 41)
2. Through dialogues with others, carefully and realistically assess the system in which they work, considering needs and abilities of various persons, the cultural and moral fabric of the organization, and political constraints and imperatives
3. Superimpose a vision of the ideal upon the real and seek organizational strategies for moving the latter toward the former.

Reflection: Developing a Vision

The importance of vision in educational leadership has been stressed by Barth (1990), Bennis (1984), Sergiovanni (1987, 1992), and others. Indeed, these scholars argue that successful administration must begin with a conception of "what might be, what could be, perhaps what should be" (Barth, 1990, p. 161). They also, though, emphasize that this vision must be coupled with a clear understanding of the realities of life in schools. Administrators seeking to establish an image of a good school and to understand how this image might be actualized in their specific situation are likely to find reflection on a range of topics helpful.

Christopher Hodgkinson (1983) underscores the importance of broad-based philosophical reflection in administration. Indeed, he suggests that this activity is critical for those leaders who simultaneously seek "a concept of the desirable" (Parsons, 1951, p. 162, quoted in Hodgkinson, 1983, p. 36) and an understanding of "organizational reality" (p. 75) and of human nature.

> The deadliest weapons in the administrative armory are philosophical; the skills of logical and critical analysis, conceptual synthesis, value analysis and commitment, the powers of expression in language and communication, rhetoric and, most fundamentally, the depth of understanding of human nature. So in the end philosophy becomes intrinsically practical. The cartography it provides becomes the administrator's most vital navigation aid. (p. 53)

Donald Schön (1983, 1984, 1987) is another advocate for reflection in and on the practice of educational administration. Distinguishing between this way of thinking and "technical rationality . . . an epistemology of practice . . . [that assumes that] rigorous professional practitioners solve well-formed instrumental problems by applying theory and technique derived from systematic, preferably scientific knowledge" (1987, pp. 3–4), Schön suggests the latter is of limited usefulness in practice. He argues that often "the problems of real-world practice do not present themselves as problems at all but as messy, indeterminate situations" (1987, p. 4) and proposes that leaders engage in a kind of thoughtful introversion, contemplating that which they do intuitively. Thinking in this manner, educators will find themselves able to make "normative judgments" (1987, p. 23) regarding their work in a manner similar to an artist who can "recognize the mismatch of an element to an overall pattern . . . without the slightest ability or need to describe in words the norms they see as violated" (1987, p. 23). In Schön's view, leaders who reflect upon their work, allowing instinct to inform and support logic, will be best able to visualize and move toward caring and effective organizational structures.

Farquhar (1970), Popper (1990), and Brieshke (1990, 1991) suggest that, in the humanities, administrators can find fodder for productive reflection especially in regard to ethical organizational strategies. Farquhar (1970) asserts that school leaders can find in literature, history, philosophy, and related fields, insight into "the essential humanity" (p. 54) of those inhabiting schools. Popper concurs, noting that the humanities offer "multiple insights into the human situation . . . [resulting in] what psychologists call empathic insight" (p. 7). Such insight, in his view, is essential if one is to conceive of structures that effectively and ethically seek to meet human needs. Focusing specifically on reflection upon novels, Brieshke (1990) notes that this activity can aid administrators in "creat[ing] new understandings" (p. 388), understandings essential for envisioning good schools.

Foster (1986a) and Starratt (1991) recommend another mode of reflective thought. Both call on leaders to critically assess organizational strategies, pedagogical methods, and the assumptions that underlie them. In Foster's view, rigorous critical thinking facilitates the ability of educators to develop alternative, genuinely transformative approaches to leadership. Calling for "a critique of positivism and the related ideas of fact–value separation and value neutrality in administration, a critique of modern rationality as it is embodied in administrative principles, and a focus on the ideas of power and liberation as concern for administration" (p. 63), he challenges thoughtful educators to identify and question assumptions underlying research conclusions and commonly accepted practices. Starratt (1991) specifically notes that this critical reflection can assist caring leaders in making organizational decisions in that it can help them distinguish between ethical and unethical practices.

Dialogue: Assessing Reality

Reflection is fundamentally a solitary process. While necessary in imagining, thinking, and planning, it—alone—is not sufficient for transforming schools. Caring leaders, recognizing that many factors influence educational operations and that schools are not solely their possessions, will seek to understand the perspective of others involved in schooling. Additionally, they will involve these persons in developing and implementing organizational strategies. To do this, they will engage in ongoing dialogues with various educational stakeholders.

Grant (1988) argues for the importance of dialogue in establishing a vision of structures consistent with fundamental beliefs of administrators, teachers, students, parents, and community members. Reflecting on Tyack and Hansot's *Managers of Virtue* (1982), he suggests that contemporary school leaders lack the sense of shared "civic and moral values" (p. 172) that guided their predecessors and that dialogue is needed to begin to identify a new set of shared values. Further, he asserts that when administrators, motivated by an ethic of caring, involve others in the process of cultivating a vision, they will, in all likelihood, discover that others desire nurturing, supportive schools and can offer important insights into ways such institutions might be organized. As an example, Grant describes some "transform[ing]" (p. 195) strategies used by principal Joseph Conan. Central to these were thought-provoking, honest interactions that promoted the development of and movement toward a shared vision.

> Conan plunged the faculty into deliberations . . . about what troubled them about the school. He began student dialogue groups. He invited parents of students who were floundering to meet with him and the teachers to talk about remedies. Out of these and other discussions came guidelines known as community rules. . . . These rules were not written in legalistic language

nor were they aimed solely at students. The community rules were a statement of expectations that all in the school community would be bound by.
They spoke of trustworthiness, honesty, fairness, competency, mutual respect,
and the responsibilities of members of a caring community. (p. 197)

The school that emerged after these and numerous other dialogical interactions
was one characterized by a high degree of commitment among teachers and
parents and the development of academic and interpersonal competency in students.

In her discussion of "goodness in high schools" (p. 309), Lightfoot (1983)
offers additional evidence supporting the value of thoughtful conversations. She
points out that principals of these schools engaged teachers in dialogues and
that they evaluated management strategies in light of these interactions.
Lightfoot notes that these interchanges may take a number of forms but that
they are inspired by the belief that teachers should be heard because they are
"the central actors in the educational process. Their satisfaction is critical to the
tone and smooth functioning of the school. Their nurturance is critical to the
nurturance of students" (p. 341). Furthermore, Lightfoot stresses that teachers
are not the only ones given a voice. Educators in these organizations possess a
"fearless and empathetic regard of students" (p. 342). They, therefore, seek to
learn more about students by talking with them and listening to them speak of
their educational needs, plans, hopes, and dreams. In Lightfoot's good schools,
visions of what institutions can and should be and realistic strategies to reach
these ideals reflect the thinking of administrators, teachers, students, parents,
alumni, and community members.

Institutionalizing Values: Structuring Opportunities to Care

An ethic of care would compel school leaders to work to move visions,
hopes, and plans beyond the conceptual stage into practice. In this effort, they
would superimpose a vision of the ideal institution upon the actual organization
and seek mechanisms to move the latter toward the former. The exact structure
of these schools would vary depending on situational needs and constraints.
Certain characteristics, however, would be common to all, for values linked to
caring would prompt administrators to focus on at least five organizational features. First, a caring ethic would prompt leaders to assert that professional educators should take the lead in defining values and in ensuring that schools support and nurture the development of all persons. Second, it would encourage
the development of nonbureaucratic decision-making school structures. Third,
this ethic would emphasize skills and competencies rather than assigned titles
as determinants of organizational roles, and it would encourage the separation
of role and status. Fourth, caring would prompt leaders to support collaborative

efforts among and between students, teachers, and administrators. Finally, this ethic would call for structures conducive to honest, ongoing communication between persons within schools and between educators and those in the larger community.

Reclaiming professional responsibility. A commitment to caring schools would compel administrators to reassess personal and professional values, thoughtfully and collaboratively to define (or redefine) success—for themselves, teachers, and students—and to guard these values and definitions, when they are challenged. It would require that leaders steadfastly resist forces that, explicitly or implicitly, equate worth and achievement, and that they work to develop a school-wide perspective that views persons as intrinsically valuable and accomplishments as signs or indicators of growth and development. Additionally, it would move administrators into the role of advocates for caring in schools.

Superintendents and principals who accept this challenge would be accepting their professional responsibility. Instead of reactively allowing perspectives from business or politics to determine educational values, these administrators would assert that their training, experience, and emotional investment in schools place them in a position to determine the ways in which persons, achievements, successes, and failures should be viewed. Indeed, they would recognize that professionalism entails confidently assuming responsibility for developing and operating under ethical values and standards. These leaders would share Dewey's (1959) view that educators, because of their training and expertise, can offer "expert service" (p. vi) to schools and larger communities. At times, this will entail "drawing . . . boundary lines that will be conducive to respect, restraint, and efficiency" (p. x), to limit inappropriate input from persons outside of education. The process of reclaiming the rights to define educational values and to act to protect those values could potentially push school leaders into conflictual situations. It is important to note that a commitment to care does not preclude involvement in such conflicts. It does, however, offer guidance for interacting in ways that respect the fundamental dignity of all. In the paragraphs that follow I suggest some strategies that might be useful to leaders desiring to reclaim the right to care in schools.

A thoughtful examination of theoretical, philosophical, and empirical works on the ethics of schooling can provide educators with evidence to support the legitimacy of caring. The writings of many (e.g., Bates, 1984; Buber, 1965; Dewey, 1959; Foster, 1984, 1986a, 1986b, 1988, 1989; Immegart & Burroughs, 1970; Mitchell & Cunningham, 1990; Noddings, 1984; Oliver, 1976; Purpel, 1989; Rich, 1971; Shea, Kahane, & Sola, 1990; Toch, 1991) contain penetrating analyses of the forces that historically have influenced education and support the importance of ethical, value-driven leadership. Both the content of these works and the authors' reasoning processes have the potential to provide leaders with systematic ways to understand, discuss, and defend their work. Indeed, as Hodgkinson (1983) reminds us, "the deadliest weapons in the administrative arsenal are philosophical" (p. 53). School officers who wish to win back the right to rethink the bases of value in schools would do well to arm themselves with these weapons.

Administrators seeking to hold to caring values might also benefit from a thoughtful study of empirical work on caring schools. As Popper (1990) notes, "in an applied field, such as Educational Administration [with] its self-affirmed preoccupation with the *practical,* one also has to lay out in clear view the *instrumental* value [of proposed innovations]" (p. 4, emphasis in the original). Chapter 3 contains references to a number of studies suggesting a correlation between a caring ethos, satisfied teachers, and student achievement. Leaders who find themselves dealing with persons who believe "a get-tough environment is the sign of a good school" (Toch, 1991, p. 237) may find that hard data are needed to challenge this type of thinking and to introduce the possibility of gentler, more nurturing strategies.

Reconceptualizing decision-making structures.   Caring administrators would not only protect this ethic from challenges, they would also actively promote it by various organizational strategies. As noted at the beginning of this chapter, educational leaders have typically operated under the assumption that schools should be bureaucracies. (See Beck & Murphy, 1993, and Campbell et al., 1987, for discussions of the origins of this assumption.) Even when structural changes have been attempted, it usually has involved altering the bureaucratic pyramid in some way, not fundamentally changing its form. Leaders, operating under the dual assumptions that each person should have a voice in decisions affecting her or him and that each possesses value regardless of title, position, or accomplishment, would promote a different governance structure. Instead of a pyramid, they would look to a circle as a model, a circle with flexible and selectively permeable boundaries. This image captures several key features of an organization developed on a foundation of caring. Within a circle, no point is in a superior position; such would be the case in caring schools. Roles with different tasks and responsibilities would exist, but none would be viewed as better or more important than others (Beare, 1989; Beck & Murphy, 1993). Further, the flexible boundaries suggest a spirit of inclusiveness that would characterize caring schools, for these communities would expand, as needed, to include students, teachers, and other appropriate persons or groups (Beck & Newman, 1992; Buber, 1965; Kirkpatrick, 1986; Louis & Miles, 1992; Macmurray, 1961). The selective permeability of these boundaries reflects a sense of administrative reality, for schools are open systems, and effective leaders will acknowledge and accept that fact (Campbell et al., 1987; Cohen & March, 1974; Mortimer & McConnell, 1978). They will also, though, realize that some forces should not be allowed in schools. Recognizing the links between those outside of schools and within schools, they will embrace parents and others who have the possibility of positively affecting the school and community and make every effort to screen out those who would exploit children, their families, and teachers for political or financial gain.

In schools organized according to a caring ethic, accomplishments would be indicators of competence, not personal or professional worth, and competence would serve as guide to the assignment or assumption of organizational roles. (This is consistent with recommendations offered by American Association of Colleges of Teacher Education, 1988; Angus, 1988; Beck & Murphy, 1993; and Murphy, 1991.) Leaders organizing according to this principle would seek to identify and respond to skills, interests, and abilities. They would also evaluate continually the needs of their school or system, a process that would require a high degree of involvement in terms of time and energy (Halpin & Croft, 1962; Sergiovanni, 1987; Vaill, 1984) and an ongoing willingness to learn. Furthermore, they would commit themselves to increasing the knowledge and skills of all school personnel, a task likely to be easier if personal and professional worth and competency are separated.

In organizing efforts, administrators guided by an ethic of care would encourage collaborative efforts between faculty, staff, and students. These would serve to promote interpersonal interactions, to deemphasize competition, to facilitate a sense of belonging, and to increase individuals' skills as they learn from one another. Additionally, the results of these group efforts would have the potential to be quite impressive because the strengths of the collaborators would be likely to complement one another, with one supplying what another lacks.

Leaders organizing for collaboration might find several strategies useful. Ashton and Webb (1986) report on their extensive comparison of "two schools that differed on three organizational dimensions . . . (1) interdisciplinary team versus department organization, (2) multi-age versus single-age grouping, and (3) adviser-advisee program versus homeroom program" (p. 26).

> Teaching teams, adviser–advisee programs, multi-aged grouping, and clear and shared educational aims appeared to lessen teachers' self-doubts and to diminish the self-protective, low efficacy ideologies that accompany such doubts. (p. 121)

Maeroff's (1990) report on Shoreham-Wading River, "a good middle school" (p. 505), tells of a similar pattern of organizing for collaboration and interaction. "A team approach insures that in each grade a core group of 40 to 54 children is taught four main subjects by a team of two teachers. . . . Collaboration is tacitly encouraged by putting the two teachers in adjoining classrooms, linked by a doorway" (p. 506).

Epstein (1990) also writes about effective, community-building organizational practices. For example, she describes one school's system of assigning students to a lunchroom table and allowing them to work together in monitoring behavior and clean-up. Additionally, reporting on the results of a survey of middle school principals, she notes that "'signature practices'" (p. 443) of good middle schools reflect a strong commitment to developing positive, supportive interactions among and between administrators, teachers, students, and parents. Epstein's support for organizational structures that encourage collaboration was reinforced by the results of a study that showed that "the single strongest predictor of the higher ratings of the quality of school programs overall is the use of common planning periods for members of interdisciplinary teams" (p. 443). Becker (1990) writes of the benefits of instituting outdoor "challenge course[s]" (p. 456) in which students and teachers work together to overcome a number of obstacles. And MacIver (1990) notes that data on "interdisciplinary [teaching] teams [and] advisory groups" (p. 464) reveal "important benefits associated with establishing extensive and well-organized implementations of these practices" (p. 464). These benefits—academic achievement, teacher commitment, and the facilitation of personal development—are quite consistent with a caring ethic's emphases.

McPartland (1990) also discusses effective collaborative "staffing patterns" (p. 468).

> Such [patterns] might include assigning each student a specific staff member as advocate or mentor and providing regularly scheduled time when students and mentors can meet to discuss the students' problems and progress. In the same vein interdisciplinary teams of teachers who share the same instructional group of students can deal with the needs of individual students if time and training are available to team members. (p. 469).

Grant (1988), in turn, tells of an effective collaborative disciplinary technique.

> Instead of being sent to the office, students violating . . . community rules . . . were sent to what became known as the "planning room." This was a form of in-school suspension, and the room was manned by teachers on rotation throughout the day in lieu of study hall or other duties. Once in the room, it was the student's responsibility to develop a plan for readmittance to the class that included giving an account of the infraction that both student and teacher found acceptable. This sometimes involved a "cooling-off" period of a day or two—although students were responsible for making up work missed in other classes while working out their plan. The teachers staffing the room

talked over the problem with the student and helped in development of a plan—often acting as go-betweens with the teachers who had originally disciplined the student. (p. 199)

One facet of effective collaborative efforts, noted by virtually all these authors, is frequent communication between participants. Such communication not only facilitates team efforts, but also contributes to the development of trust between those involved (Beck & Newman, 1992; Buber, 1958, 1965; Habermas, 1984, 1988; Fromm, 1956). Recommendations for structuring schools to encourage communication are often presented as ways to promote collegiality. Again, administrative literature offers a number of practical strategies. The observations of Maeroff (1990) suggest a strategy for enhancing communication. Focusing on teacher-student interchanges, he recommends that administrators consider developing an advisory program that allows a single adult to spend a great deal of time with only a few students. Carrying this concept further, Noddings (1988, 1992) suggests that groups of students stay with the same teacher for a period of least three years.

Louis and Miles's (1992) case studies on two large urban high schools that, in the past decade, have shown marked improvements in a number of areas, contain descriptions of activities school site leaders might wish to emulate. In both, the ability to change was linked to increased, productive communication between educators, and, in both, principals did much to encourage this process. Mark Cohen of Agassiz High School in Boston concentrated on "strengthening social bonds among teachers and administrators" (p. 78) in the belief this would enhance working relationships. To that end he supported "staff parties and a Christmas dance" (p. 70) along with other efforts to bring faculty together. Cara Mosley of Alameda High School in Los Angeles, along with several teachers, scheduled a voluntary retreat for teachers and administrators to allow them to step back from the day-to-day activities and talk with one another about students' needs and their own concerns. This spawned additional retreats and led to school-wide commitment to keep classroom doors open to facilitate knowledge and support peers and to alleviate teachers' sense of isolation.

THE CARING ADMINISTRATOR
AS CREATIVE AND CAPABLE PEDAGOGUE

Early in the history of educational administration, persons who filled leadership roles considered themselves to be, first and foremost, teachers. In the early part of this century, the emphasis shifted from pedagogy to management, and school leaders began to look to business for models and methods (Beck &

Murphy, 1993; Button, 1966; Callahan, 1962; Campbell et al., 1987; Tyack & Hansot, 1982). Recently, theorists and practitioners alike have begun to focus, again, on the administrator as an instructional leader (Evans, 1989; Greenfield, 1987; Murphy, 1990d, 1990e; Murphy, Hallinger, Lotto, & Miller, 1987). Administrators guided by an ethic of care would certainly embrace this role, for they would recognize that schools promoting optimum development would be those in which students are taught well. These leaders would enter into the pedagogical arena determined to be caring, capable, and creative. This would, in all likelihood, mean that administrators would:

1. View themselves as learners and continually strive to develop their knowledge and skill base
2. Consider themselves to be teachers and work to transform interactions into pedagogical opportunities
3. Function as skillful managers so as to promote teaching effectiveness
4. Function as colleagues to teachers in supervision and evaluation.

Learning: The Core of Administrative Work

Central to the notion of instructional leadership is the idea that administrators should be "head learner[s]" (Barth, 1990, p. 513). One area in which ongoing learning must occur revolves around understanding teaching and learning processes. Administrators seeking to bolster, support, and enhance instructional programs certainly would seek as much knowledge as possible about this topic. This knowledge could, then, be used to plan humane, effective programs and curricula, to guide and support teachers' efforts, and to assist in devising individual instructional plans when needed. Information from experts in a variety of fields could provide important and useful knowledge. For instance, administrators seeking to promote an instructional climate conducive to cognitive, emotional, moral, and social development might benefit from studying the work of developmental psychologists. Examining a range of theories should help educators understand the complexity of this process. Additionally, it might help them establish some sense of normal and abnormal development. It could alert them to age-appropriate teaching techniques and curricula and could help administrators work with teachers in identifying and helping developmentally disabled students.

In addition to learning about growth and development, caring administrators would also be concerned with discovering how to best educate an increasingly heterogeneous group of students. Schools of the next decade and beyond, consistent with the "changing nature of the [American] social fabric" (Beck & Murphy, 1993, p. 179), will contain students from a variety of races, socioeconomic levels, and family backgrounds (Carnegie Council on Adolescent Development, 1989; Kirst, McLaughlin, & Massell, 1990; Wagstaff & Gallagher, 1990). These students will present educators with complex personal and social situations, and with varied attitudes toward schooling (Conroy, 1972; Freedman, 1990; Kidder, 1989; Levine, 1987; Rose, 1989; Wagstaff & Gallagher, 1990). Coping with this diversity will compel caring leaders to learn as much as possible about cultural, social, and individual variables affecting learning. Developing cultural sensitivity, in all likelihood, will require that they go beyond academic work on these topics and seek ways to immerse themselves in the worlds of others, listening to and learning from a range of persons. In addition to pursuing opportunities for lived experiences, administrators might find the thoughtful examination of novels and films helpful in this effort.

As they seek to learn about the contexts within which schools are situated, caring administrators also would seek information on ways to work with each and every youngster in their schools. Parents are potentially an important source of knowledge in this area. Experts from the community—pediatricians, child psychologists, and the like—might also be helpful. If the child has had previous successful experiences in any kind of educational environment, the teachers who worked with that child might also provide valuable insights.

Another area of potential learning relates to facilitating the personal and professional growth of faculty colleagues. In this effort, administrators could learn much from examining theoretical and empirical work on teachers and teaching. For example, understanding the interrelationship between teachers' ideologies, expectations, and feelings of effectiveness (Ashton & Webb, 1986) would help leaders to sensitively work with frustrated, "burned-out" faculty. Contemplating the practical and philosophical problems related to tracking (Oakes, 1985) or the benefits of cooperative learning (Aljose & Joyner, 1990; Johnson & Johnson, 1989; Slavin, 1980, 1983) could guide administrators in organizing for just, caring, *and* effective teaching. And understanding the complex array of social forces that affect classroom events (Schmuck & Schmuck, 1988) could provide leaders with a broad, macro-level understanding of schooling, an understanding that could help place specific strategies in a larger, more informed perspective.

In addition to examining literature, caring instructional leaders would listen to and learn directly from teachers. Rallis (1990) emphasizes the importance of principals and teachers engaging in "a dialogue about what is to be taught and how it is to be taught, as well as how teaching is to be judged" (p. 196). Darling-Hammond (1988) agrees. Emphasizing that principals should be open to teachers' insights, she writes, "Effective teaching is not routine, students are not passive, and questions of practice are not simple, predictable, or standardized. Consequently, instructional decisions cannot be formulated on high, then packaged, and handed down to teachers" (quoted in Rallis, 1990, p. 196).

Ashton and Webb (1986) offer additional data supporting the importance of administrators' talking with, listening to, and learning from teachers. For instance, they report on a project (Joyce, Hersh, & McKibbon, 1983) in which "a group of teachers, administrators, [and] parents" (p. 165) worked together to foster instructional excellence. Ashton and Webb describe the results of this effort.

> Teachers [were] consulted, their ideas [were] taken seriously, and their worries [were] taken into account. Channels of communication [were] opened and barriers of isolation [were] lowered. Responsibilities [were] shared, and staff members [began] to see, through their own experiences, that the quality of education [could] be elevated and the conditions of teaching improved. (p. 165).

Ashton and Webb's description alludes to an important feature of productive administrator–teacher interactions: They must be substantive, honest, realistic, and respectful. If such interactions are to occur, all stakeholders must recognize that issues of power and control and of roles and responsibilities must be addressed. Further, all must recognize that the process of resolving tensions is an ongoing one, characterized, at times, by discussions leading to consensus; at other times, by negotiation resulting in compromise; and, occasionally, by agreements to respect one another in the face of unresolved conflicts and disagreements. Caring administrators will enter into dialogues with a commitment to pursue consensus in a manner that honors the dignity of their teaching colleagues. (See Cuban, 1988, for a discussion of various approaches to constructive dialogical interactions.)

Often overlooked (Berliner, 1976), students can be another valuable source of information about effective instructional techniques. Weinstein (1983) offers a thorough review of research that has sought to explore teaching from the child's perspective. She notes that students' perceptions of teaching and teachers have been shown to affect classroom processes and yet, "as Hartrup (1979) suggests, our knowledge of this realm of experience is shockingly incomplete" (p. 288). Weinstein reviews research that offers insights into students' perceptions of teachers, classroom behaviors and pedagogical strategies, students' views of their peers and the interactions between social climates and learning, their understandings of causes of their own and others' behaviors, and students' self-perceptions. She suggests that such data collected in these various investigative efforts should be studied by those interested in instructional effectiveness. It is not inconsistent to suggest that, in addition to studying formal research, administrators should engage in informal efforts to talk with and to learn from students.

Pedagogy: A Central Administrative Activity

In addition to being learners, caring administrators would also function as teachers in that they would view personal and professional interactions as opportunities to further educative purposes, embracing whatever roles these purposes required. Evans (1989, 1991a, 1991b) uses the words "socially aware and pedagogically responsive" (1991a, p. 4) to describe such leaders. After thoughtfully analyzing stories of practice told by nine principals, he suggests that "the . . . pedagogic character of educational administra[tion]" has moved from a dominant to a "latent" (1991a, p. 2) place in thought and practice. Evans argues against this change and asserts that certain activities are needed if the adjective "educational" is to be restored to its rightful place in the title "educational administrator." Some of the activities he discusses relate to administrator preparation and will be discussed in Chapter 6. Others, however, have direct implications for practitioners.

The first of these involves a fundamental reorientation of leaders in regard to their work. Evans notes that "for educational administration to become a strong practice with the capacity to contribute seriously to the work of educators, it needs to be reconstituted from the ground up as a pedagogic practice" (1991b, p. 17). This reconstitution would, in his view, be facilitated if educators would turn their attention from "technical admonitions, prescriptive formulae and the like" (p. 17) and focus on the traditional and historical bases of their work. "The important point to be made is that the development of a pedagogically-oriented educational administration does not yield a new or hitherto unknown practice. Rather it yields to the practice that truly belongs to it, and what constitutes its ground and first moment" (p. 17).

In order to be a pedagogical leader of students, an administrator/teacher would need to be visible, available, understanding, and supportive. Epstein (1990), Evans (1989, 1991a, 1991b), and Grant (1988) offer examples of ways this might be accomplished. Epstein, for example, describes an "exemplary" principal engaged in "many daily one-to-one interactions" (p. 439) with students, and she writes of principals and assistant principals who roam halls and classes—not to maintain order—but to have more time for informal interactions with young people. Analyzing "nine administrative situations or life-world stories drawn from interviews with practicing school principals" (1991a, p. 1), Evans discusses ways these leaders might have conducted interactions with greater pedagogical effectiveness. He especially emphasizes that administrators need to understand the perspectives and values of others, something that may require temporarily suspending their own understanding of a situation (see also Noddings, 1984). Grant describes another caring, pedagogically oriented administrator. "He visited students in the hospital and took school-work to the homes of those who had been suspended to show that discipline was not born of hatred. He had the capacity to engage the students, faculty, and parents in dialogue about the issues that really mattered" (p. 197).

Administrators, committed to caring and effective instructional leadership, would encourage the ongoing professional development of all within their school. Attempting to stay abreast of research on such topics as child and adolescent development, on innovative teaching strategies, and on effective disciplinary techniques, leaders would seek to communicate this information to their faculties in tactful, supportive ways. They would continually bear in mind that all are professionals and that, in schools that are caring communities, adults mutually and reciprocally support one another's professional development. Sergiovanni and Starratt (1988) actually suggest a specific technique administrators might use to approach teachers in a caring and respectful manner. Noting that when "individual teachers are unaware of inconsistencies between their espoused theories and their theories in use, they are not likely to search for alternatives to their present teaching patterns" (p. 365), these authors recommend a technique called "surfacing dilemmas" (p. 365). Instructional leaders taking this approach would not take a heavy-handed authoritarian approach and attempt to mandate changes in methods and curricula. Instead, they would discuss observed inconsistencies in an effort to provoke teachers into thinking about new and different strategies. As teachers began to seek more appropriate and effective approaches, administrators, possessing a knowledge of "teaching and professional practice alternatives" (p. 366) could support and guide as needed.

Management: Facilitating the Instructional Program

Emphasizing the educative dimensions of their work does not mean instructional leaders would abandon managerial tasks. Indeed, the dual roles of educator and administrator would compel them to focus on external, environmental conditions that either facilitate or hinder instruction (Murphy, 1988). Leaders committed to caring and competency would seek, in appropriate ways, to cultivate favorable learning conditions. Many managerial strategies have been discussed in the previous section as organizational strategies; others will be discussed in the final section. Therefore, I only touch on the topic here, suggesting general roles and activities that might be useful. Caring instructional leaders would look not to profit-driven CEOs, but to environmental engineers as models. Taking an ecological approach, these leaders would seek

> not to bend individual behavior to conform to externally imposed notions of school improvement, but, rather, to transform schools so that they no longer alienate teachers, administrators, and students, and to free the intelligence of

those who work in schools, so they might better analyze their problems, invent solutions, and improve the quality of education. (Ashton & Webb, 1986, p. 161).

Berry and Ginsberg (1990) describe activities characteristic of ecologically sensitive leader/managers. These include "seizing initiative, actively exploiting resources, supporting teacher projects, spreading good news about the school, and short-cutting the bureaucracy, . . . articulating a vision, possessing coping skills for decisive and quick action, and managing the external environment" (p. 167). Morris, Crowson, Porter-Gehrie, and Horowitz (1983) suggest that this management would take school site administrators out of their offices and into the schools.

> A busy principal covers a great deal of ground. In making these rounds, from office to corridor to classroom to gymnasium to boiler room to playground and back, the principal is managing the school. But it is management in a form unusual for most organizations because it is, in large part, administration at the work stations of other persons. (p. 211)

Administrators motivated by an ethic of care would exert appropriate control of the school environment so that healthy growth—for all persons—in all areas is possible.

Supervision and Evaluation: Acting as Professional Colleagues

Two leadership tasks invariably affecting the instructional climate are supervision and evaluation of teachers. An ethic of care would influence administrators' understanding of purposes, processes, and roles in these activities. In recent years, supervision and evaluation have been viewed as activities for monitoring teachers' work, judging their effectiveness based on student outcomes, and meting out rewards for "success" and punishments for "failures" (see, e.g., National Governors' Association, 1986; United States Department of Education, 1989; Wise, 1989). Administrators guided by caring would reject these purposes, viewing them as patronizing, discouraging of teacher professionalism, and ineffective in achieving desired results. Instead, they would consider supervision and evaluation as activities intended to promote personal and professional development and well-being (Sergiovanni & Starratt, 1988). Viewing these as endeavors to support teaching and learning, caring instructional leaders would be considerate and fundamentally noncritical. With teachers, they would assume the roles of professional colleagues, co-learners, supportive counselors, and friends. Furthermore, they would seek to be understanding listeners, creative problem solvers, and, when necessary, mediators or advocates.

Formulating this type of understanding would, in all likelihood, require that leaders engage in thoughtful reflection and dialogue. Because these activities have been discussed in some detail throughout this chapter, I focus here on ways they might specifically influence thinking about supervision and evaluation. Sergiovanni and Starratt's (1988) words are especially instructive. They suggest that administrators and teachers alike would benefit from reflecting on the "ordinariness" of these processes. Indeed, they write that these are "common and inescapable aspect[s] of most of what we do—whether we are buying shoes, selecting a vacation sport, redecorating the living room, enjoying a movie, football game, or art show" (p. 351). These authors state that, in day-to-day life, these activities are intended "to discern, understand, and appreciate; to judge, value, and decide" (p. 351) and that, in education, they have similar purposes. Administrators holding this demystified view of supervision and evaluation should be better able to remember that these activities are intended to understand and support teachers and teaching, to celebrate effective instructional approaches, and to collaboratively solve problems and discover new and better ways to promote learning and development.

This conception of purposes would influence the manner in which administrators actually supervise and evaluate their colleagues. Indeed, a concern for understanding and supporting teachers would prompt leaders to avoid entering the supervisory transaction with preconceived notions about what and how teachers should be teaching. For example, Beck and Newman (1992) found that caring principals tended to define success as growth, and definitions of both growth and success were developed by involved parties in a collaborative manner. Their findings support Barth's (1990) contention that "list logic" (p. 36), the assumption that good pedagogy can be captured in lists and that persons can be measured against these "prescriptions" (p. 40), does little to improve instruction. Sergiovanni and Starratt (1988) concur and argue that, rather than depending on "pre-existing standards" (p. 351), caring supervisor/evaluators will thoughtfully observe classroom activities as often and unobtrusively as possible. Cuban (1988), citing McLaughlin and others, offers yet another approach to evaluation and supervision. Noting that "another approach to accountability is to simply render and account," he recommends that administrators and teachers jointly describe "what occurs in classrooms and schools." As these descriptions are developed, Cuban suggests that "exemplars [can be] recognized; misfits and incompetents [can be] handled . . . forthrightly and fairly" (p. 247).

When discussing observations with teachers, caring instructional leaders would seek ways to recognize and celebrate pedagogical successes. These would include measurable improvements in students' abilities and more subtle classroom "victories"—the improvement of a student's self-esteem, a well-executed team teaching effort, and the like. Freedman's *Small Victories: The Real World of a Teacher, Her Students, & Their High School* (1990) provides wonderful examples of administrators who both recognize and overlook teachers' accomplishments and reveals the powerful impact of both responses on morale and motivation. Barth (1990), in turn, tells of a discovery he made as a principal when he asked a young teacher to devise a fire escape plan. He reports that delegating this task and celebrating its accomplishment resulted in this teacher happily assuming an important leadership role in the school. Indeed, Barth suggests that a wise and caring leadership strategy is to give teachers "credit for success" (p. 138) and to "shar[e] responsibility for failure" (p. 137).

Barth's point about sharing responsibility for failure hints at another dimension of supervision and evaluation guided by a caring ethic. Leaders operating in this manner would view perceived problems as opportunities not for rebuke, but rather for constructive collaboration. Sergiovanni and Starratt's (1988) suggestion that "surfacing dilemmas" (p. 365) might be useful in dealing with inconsistencies was discussed earlier. Other caring and effective approaches for problem solving might be derived from an examination of organizational literature that focuses on collaborative management–staff relationships (e.g., Argyris, 1957, 1962; Likert, 1961, 1967; McGregor, 1960). Scholarship that explores ways teachers enlist students in solving classroom problems (e.g., DeCharms, 1972; Deci, 1971; Koenigs, Fiedler, & DeCharms, 1977) might also be helpful, providing models for administrator–teacher interactions.

Caring leaders might also promote some fundamental changes in supervisory and evaluative assumptions and methods. As discussed earlier, they might actively work to change the pervasive belief that effective teaching can be readily quantified and measured and push for multiple approaches to assess the successes of schools, teachers, and students. These leaders might also shift responsibility for supervision to teachers. This could be done through the development of mentoring programs (Barth, 1990; Rallis, 1990); through encouraging teachers to set goals, choose curricula, and devise evaluation strategies (Ashton & Webb, 1986; Rallis, 1990); through the support of teachers' professional organizations (Wise, 1989); and through relinquishing control of issues such as hiring (Wise, 1989), "salary, tenure, [and] forms of promotion" (Clark & Meloy, 1989, p. 292). Further, caring leaders might consider subjecting themselves to some form of supervision and evaluation by inviting teachers, students, parents, and other administrators to help them improve professional practice.

THE CARING ADMINISTRATOR
AS CULTIVATOR OF NURTURING CULTURES

In recent years, school culture and climate have been popular topics in educational literature. Approaching these topics from many perspectives, scholars have produced a plethora of theories, recommendations, and hypotheses. Two thematic threads running through much of this work in the area have important implications for administrators. The first of these is that the culture of a school has important and far-reaching effects on the thinking and actions of students and teachers. The second is that administrators can do much to shape, define, sustain, or change a school's culture. Leaders seeking to operate under a caring ethic surely would seek to cultivate a culture where such an ethic could flourish. In doing this they might find it helpful to pay attention to the following dimensions of cultural influence (see Bolman & Deal, 1984, 1991, for a fuller discussion of these).

1. Metaphors used by administrators can have a powerful impact on the assumptions and beliefs of teachers, parents, students, and community members.
2. The telling of stories, myths, and legends can help to define cultural values and to inspire organizational members to strive for these values.
3. Meanings are often more important than actual events in shaping culture.
4. Rituals, ceremonies, and celebrations give organizational members an opportunity to corporately express needs, hopes, and values.

Using Metaphors: Cultural Currency of Caring Cultures

In recent years, metaphors have been of great interest to students of organizations. In his seminal *Images of an Organization* (1986), Gareth Morgan explores metaphors persons use in understanding their institutions and the ways these affect actions and decisions. Noting that "theories and explanations of organizational life are based upon metaphors that lead us to see and understand organizations in distinctive yet practical ways" (p. 12), Morgan asserts that figurative language simultaneously expands and limits the perspective of organizational participants. Patina (1988) and Perrin (1987) concur with this assessment. The former notes that figurative language can lead to a "highlighted interpretation" (p. 22; see also Bredeson, 1985, 1987, 1988) of events. In turn, Perrin states, "Metaphor opens us to experience in certain ways and closes us in others. It invites us to participate in the constitution of reality while, at the same time, barring us from the consideration of rival alternatives" (p. 265).

Bates (1984) offers an articulate discussion of the powerful, but often unrecognized, impact of metaphors on the culture of schools.

> Metaphors profoundly, and often unconsciously, determine our attitudes toward the world, people, events, and actions. Teachers and administrators and

their pupils use metaphors continually to represent relationships and to define the power structure which organize behavior. Metaphor is a major weapon in the presentation of self and the management of situations. . . .

Metaphors not only intrude on the processes of educational administration in a grand fashion as in the language of cybernetics, they also directly affect our negotiations and relations with each other at the most personal level. (p. 265)

Building on this theoretical framework, Bredeson (1985, 1987, 1988) and Kelley and Bredeson (1987) explore the impact of principals' metaphors on role expectations, leadership actions, and organizational culture and conclude that figurative language reveals and shapes the latter three.

Educational literature abounds with examples of the types of figurative language that might be used by a leader concerned with a caring school culture. Reflecting on his own experiences as a practitioner, Roland Barth (1990) notes that he consciously attempted to use words that would distinguish between his vision of transformed schools and the stereotypical institution. He describes avoiding "PTA rhetoric . . . words like discipline, rigor, works, basics, standards. All harsh, legitimate sounding words that revealed less of [his] personal vision and more of what [he] thought parents and others wanted to hear" (p. 149), and seeking, instead, metaphors that conveyed a sense of caring and supportive school communities.

Grant's (1988) words offer other examples of transformative leaders' use of language. Writing of two schools with "a strong positive ethos" (p. 166), he states:

Another characteristic [that] these schools shared [was that] both were led by women and had virtually all-female faculties. This is not to argue that male faculties are uncaring, but to suggest that these women, to use Carol Gilligan's language, spoke "in a different voice." (p. 178)

Grant's descriptions make it clear that these women, in a literal sense, tended to use the language of caring. He quotes an administrator as she discussed a troubled student: "Please watch out for her, help her balance her life, help her in that fragile balance" (p. 178). Underscoring the fact that this "feminine" language is not a monopoly of women, Grant also writes of a male leader who helped to develop a caring culture: "He rejected the language of modern management techniques. Conan was unashamed to talk to the faculty about 'love of mankind' or to ask, 'If we are not here to serve people, what else is there in life?'" (p. 196)

Starratt (1991) also underscores the importance of metaphors in a caring culture. Discussing ways an administrator might cultivate a caring tone, he writes:

Often the use of language in official communiques will tell the story. Formal abstract language is the language of bureaucracy, of distance; humor, familiar imagery and metaphor, and personalized messages are the language of caring. (pp. 196–197)

Storytelling: Creating, Sustaining, and Developing Values

Stories, myths, and legends are, in a sense, expanded metaphors, and, like metaphors, they are able to reveal and shape culture. In the foreword to Witherell and Noddings's *Stories Lives Tell: Narrative and Dialogue in Education* (1991), Maxine Greene underscores the power of narratives.

Jerome Bruner wrote that "narrative deals with the vicissitudes of human intentions" and identified storytelling as a human mode of thought (1986, pp. 16ff). Alisdair MacIntyre has stressed the fact that actions become intelligible when human beings tell about their intentions; "narrative history," he said, "of a certain kind turns out to be the basic and essential genre for the characterization of human actions" (1981, p. 194). More recently, Charles Taylor has written that "because we cannot but orient ourselves to the good and thus determine our place relative to it, . . . we must inescapably understand our lives in narrative form, as a 'quest'" (1989, pp. 51–52). (p. ix)

Bolman and Deal (1984, 1991) concur, noting that stories often take on mythical dimensions in organizations—especially those which deal with the development of institutional purposes or the activities or qualities of admirable participants. Arguing that these myths serve multiple purposes, these authors assert that effective leaders will know their institutions' mythology and, further, that they will tell and retell these in ways that promote desired ends. Starratt (1991), in turn, suggests that good educational administrators see dramatic narratives in even mundane events and that they inspire and energize their colleagues by helping them see this side of schooling (see also Sergiovanni & Starratt, 1988).

Administrators interested in promoting a caring, community-oriented school culture could find storytelling a helpful activity. Numerous phenomena might serve as inspiration and guides for those seeking to develop a repertoire of narratives. Schubert (1991) suggests that "teacher lore" (p. 207) should have a prominent place in the conversations of theorists and practitioners. This phrase refers to "the experiential knowledge that informs . . . teaching, [knowledge often] . . . reveal[ed] through stories about . . . practical experience" (p. 208). Schubert's words are reminiscent of Schön's reminder that novice teachers are most likely to grow as reflective, ethical "senior practitioners . . . initiate them into the traditions of practice" (1987, pp. 16–17). As experienced administrators seek to encourage the development of less experienced colleagues, they may find telling and retelling tales of actual, ideal, or possible practice to be a useful initiation strategy.

Stories of the history and traditions of a school could also help to establish a normative sense of the organization's mission and purpose. Deal and Peterson (1990) offer a helpful example of a principal who used narratives of the past to help establish a vision for the future. Hank Cotton assumed the principalship of a school experiencing excessive absenteeism, a marked lack of discipline, and a proliferation of courses with little academic substance. These seemed to reflect a general malaise and apathy on the part of students, teachers, and parents who felt disengaged from the school community. Cotton engaged in a number of activities, with varying degrees of success. One that was especially effective was the use of stories to develop a distinctive culture. "He told stories about innovation, hard work, and the many ways that teachers made a difference in the lives of students" (quoted in Bolman & Deal, 1991, p. 400).

Cotton's use of literature hints at a dimension of storytelling in education discussed at length by Susan Resnick Parr in *The Moral of the Story: Literature, Values, and American Education* (1982). Arguing that school leaders, since the 1960s, have generally overlooked the "moral and values dimensions" (p. xv) of education, Parr contends that stories, used in classrooms, faculty meetings, and schools as a whole, can provide excellent springboards for discussions of moral issues and dilemmas. Burlingame (1984) suggests that stories of "contrived situation[s]" (p. 299) may have similar results. He recommends presenting faculty members with open-ended tales of moral dilemmas and, with them, discussing possible resolutions and the processes by which they are reached.

Persons who embody educational values—"heroes and heroines" (Bolman & Deal, 1991, p. 257)—might also be the subjects of narratives. Lightfoot (1983) tells of one administrator's use of this type of story. She writes of the high attendance figures at John F. Kennedy, a large inner city high school, and cites "the inspired work of the attendance office . . . run by David Epstein, an energetic empathetic figure with an unusual magnetism" (p. 94) as a major reason for success in this area. Lightfoot discusses Epstein's attitudes and actions and notes that he was an articulate storyteller. In her view, Epstein's use of stories about actual and fictional figures, who had faced and overcome substantial difficulties, helped to instill in students a belief that success was, indeed, a possibility for them.

R. F. Delderfield's *To Serve Them All My Days* (1972) contains a powerful example of a fictional administrator's story of a somewhat unconventional school hero. In this novel, set in an English boarding school between the two World Wars, Algernon Herries, the caring and compassionate headmaster of Bamfylde School, retires. At the farewell dinner honoring him, he tells a story about someone who, in his view, exemplifies the school's ideas.

> It was a very trivial incident, but it must have impressed me at the time. Why else should it have stayed in the mind for nearly twenty years? It concerned two boys, Petherick and "Chuff" Rodgers, who accompanied me over to Bar-

combe by train, when we were giving a charity performance for that year's opera. It was Christmas time, of course, and the train was very full. We finally secured seats in a compartment where a young woman was nursing a baby. Within minutes of starting out the baby was dramatically sick. . . . I remember poor Petherick's expression well as he took refuge behind my copy of *The Times.* Upside down it was, but a thing like that wouldn't bother Petherick. He was one of our sky-rockets, and went on to become president of a famous insurance company and collect the O. B. E., or whatever they give the cream of insurance brokers. But I wasn't thinking so much of Petherick but of Chuff. Always unlucky, he had been sitting alongside the mother and was thus on the receiving end of the business. I didn't know what to do, but Chuff did. He whipped out a handkerchief—the only clean handkerchief I'd ever seen him sport—leaned across, wiped the baby's face and then the mother's lap. And when I say "wiped," I mean wiped. It wasn't a dab. It was more of a general tidy-up, all around. After that we had a tolerably uneventful journey, with Rodgers making soothing noises all the way to the junction. (pp. 286–287)

Noting that Rodgers, who was killed in World War I, never achieved prosperity in the traditional sense of that word, Herries comments, "I thought of him as one of our outstanding successes" (p. 287). Chuff Rodgers embodied the values Herries supported at Bamfylde. By telling stories such as this, he conveyed these values to others.

Attending to Meanings: Interpreting Acts and Events

The meanings underlying events and activities would also be a concern of cultural leaders. Indeed, wise administrators would realize that the symbolic dimensions of their actions and decisions have incredible power to influence organizational culture. Those seeking to cultivate a spirit of caring would seriously consider Hirsch and Andrews's (1984) observation that "an important aspect of administrative leadership consists of knowing which set of symbols to invoke at different points in time" (p. 170). They would, thus, cultivate a sensitivity to the symbolic impact of the schedule and programmatic decisions, physical layout and use of the school, and disciplinary strategies.

Recently several scholars have begun to challenge assumptions that have often guided scheduling and program decisions, asserting that traditional ways of planning have focused on efficiency and have neglected personal and relational needs of teachers and students (see, e.g., Noddings, 1984, 1988; Purpel, 1989; Toch, 1991). Many issuing these challenges propose alternative instructional arrangements or programs that, in their view, more adequately address these needs. Noddings (1988) and Sizer (1985), for example, call on administrators to consider ways to provide "extended [consistent] contact" (Noddings,

1988, p. 225) between individual teachers and small groups of students. Purpel (1989) focuses on the need for "a curriculum for social justice and compassion" (p. 121), a concept also explored by Higgins (1989) and Martin (1989), who discuss programs that might prove useful in cultivating "creative caring . . . [and] 'imaginative helping'" (Martin, 1989, p. 183) in schools. Toch (1991), decrying "the regulatory aspects of the excellence agenda" (p. 270), asserts that leaders must seek positive motivation strategies for both teachers and students.

Each of these recommendations, in addition to having "actual" effects, has great symbolic potential, for each conveys a message about administrative values and commitments. Sizer (1985) emphasizes symbolic dimensions of administrative actions. He offers a number of recommendations to educational leaders, many of which are entirely consistent with a caring ethic, and suggests that the symbolic impact of adopting these recommendations could be quite powerful in promoting a transformed culture. Indeed, he proposes that teachers' beliefs that they are respected, trusted, and efficacious are central mediating variables between organizational changes and the ability of those changes to produce desired outcomes.

Focusing on teacher–student interactions, Noddings (1988) makes a similar point. She suggests that "establishing settings more conducive to caring and, thus, to moral education" (p. 226) would have a rather immediate impact on interactions in schools. She also notes, though, that caring instructional arrangements would have important symbolic effects. They would convey to students the fact that they are known and cared for as persons with a unique set of hopes, fears, desires, and abilities. Furthermore, such arrangements, in Noddings's view, would begin to change the way educators think and "allow us to embrace older priorities, newly criticized and defined, and work toward an educational system proudly oriented toward the development of decent, caring, loved, and loving persons" (p. 226).

In addition to paying attention to the symbolic dimensions of instructional arrangements, administrators might wish to consider ways the physical layout might support or hinder a caring culture. The idea that architecture, decorations, desk placement, and landscaping plans can influence educational events is not a new one to administrators. Especially since World War II, when an upsurge in building to accommodate more students occurred, educational leaders have received planning advice from several quarters. Frequently, this advice has focused on ways the physical plant can foster efficiency and economy (Callahan, 1962). Case studies of nurturing, supportive school communities suggest that planning and usage principles can also promote caring institutions. Lightfoot's (1983) description of the physical layout of John F. Kennedy High School and her conclusions about the links between the uses of the physical plant and the school's ethos are informative. She describes an unlocked auditorium in which groups of students and teachers engaged in a range of activities and notes that, according to the principal, this room was deliberately left open to symbolize trust and the commitment to creative, exploratory learning. Lightfoot discovered that, in many respects, the principal's attitude toward the auditorium was mirrored by teachers in their classrooms. She writes that their chief concern in decision making is student welfare, not the appearance of such decisions to the outside world. And she notes that placing real needs above reputation appears to have encouraged a humane and caring school culture.

David Elkind (1987) offers other observations about ways a school's appearance can reveal and influence institutional culture. Taking an iconoclastic stance, he suggests that the presence of computers in classes for young children sends powerful and possibly harmful messages to students, parents, and teachers.

> The introduction of personal computers has, in many ways, provided still another domain for the use of children as symbols of leisure class status and for parental competitiveness. In addition, it has confounded the ideas about the importance of early-childhood education with the assumption that "computer literacy" at an early age is the royal road to a successful career in postindustrial society. (p. 85)

Elkind believes that the problems associated with an overemphasis on computer literacy are real. He does suggest, however, that the presence of these machines in prominent places in elementary schools symbolically underscores the belief that technological achievement, leading ultimately to success in the workplace, is more important than a celebration of the personhood of the child. He recommends that schools feature, instead, arenas where children can devise their own kinds of creative play and where the emphasis is on relating to living things—other children, teachers, and even animals—rather than to objects. Elkind proposes that such schools convey the message that children are valued for who they are, not what they do, and that relating to others in kind and supportive ways is of great educational importance.

Administrators certainly do not have total control over their facility. They can, however, influence at least some aspects of the physical appearance of the school plant and, in so doing, they can reinforce a caring ethos. They might wish to evaluate, for example, the impact of the prominent display of trophies, pictures of athletic teams, and honor rolls. Additionally, they might consider the impact of various decorating strategies. One wonders about the message to non-Christian children when Christmas or Easter decorations deck halls and classes—or the message to children from "nontraditional" families when library books, texts, plays, and such tell of two-parent, middle-class families. Leaders might also consider the effect of displaying the best samples of art, writing, or the like. Often this is done to encourage excellence, and yet the blow to the self-esteem of those whose work is not shown may not justify such a strategy.

Administrators seeking to cultivate caring would also do well to consider the impact of their disciplinary strategies. Indeed, in this area educational leaders may have their greatest opportunity to express their respect and valuing of each person—regardless of that person's actions. Curwin and Mendler (1989), in their *Discipline with Dignity,* underscore the importance of administrative actions in this sphere. These authors note that many disciplinary approaches involve "attacks on [student] dignity" (p. 10) and that these have negative effects on student and teacher morale and achievement and tend to perpetuate rather than stop behavior problems. Citing Rutter, Maughan, Mortimore, Ouston, and Smith (1979), they note, for example, that " high levels of corporal punishment and frequent disciplinary interventions" (p. 11) negatively affect students' self-esteem and result in increased misbehavior, misbehavior often exhibited in inappropriate and hurtful interactions with others. In contrast, administrators who take steps to prevent problems and, when they do occur, to approach the offenders with kindness and respect are likely to find themselves in more caring, less troubleprone schools.

Curwin and Mendler offer several specific recommendations to administrators. They, for instance, suggest that a "responsibility model" (p. 25) is more effective and ethical than an "obedience model" (p. 23). Concerning the latter, they write, "We define obedience as following rules without question, regardless of philosophical beliefs, ideas of right and wrong, instincts and experiences, or values. A student 'does it' because he is told to do it" (p. 23). In contrast, the responsibility model emphasizes that every person, student, and teacher is capable of making decisions and assuming responsibility and that the simple fact of personhood entitles each to act as a moral, responsible agent (see also Cohen, 1990). Educators holding this model would focus educational efforts on developing students' abilities to act ethically and responsibly. These leaders would, therefore, stress self-discipline and involve students in establishing expectations and the ways they might be reached.

Examples of ways leaders might promote this type of atmosphere have been noted by Beck and Newman (1992), Grant (1988), Lightfoot (1983), Maeroff (1990), Rutter and co-authors (1979), and others. Several threads run through these examples. For example, in them, students requiring disciplinary attention are viewed as community members in need of special attention and care. Furthermore, these authors report that adults typically handle problems (and those creating them) with confidence, kindness, empathy, and humor. Praise also figured prominently in the activities of caring leaders as described by Beck and Newman (1992), Rutter and co-authors (1979), and Curwin and Mendler (1989).

Participating in Rituals and Ceremonies:
Reinforcing and Celebrating Values

A culturally sensitive leader would also consider the impact of ceremonies, rituals, and celebrations in her or his school. Bolman and Deal (1991) underscore the importance of these events. "Rituals reflect and express an organization's culture—the pattern of beliefs, values, practices, and artifacts that define for its members who they are and how they do things" (p. 250). Harvey Cox (1965) offers a similar perspective. He argues that "saga, play, . . . celebration, . . . festival, and fantasy" (p. 13) are central, but often neglected, dimensions of personal and organizational life. Cox proposes that healthy and moral cultures depend on persons' being able to express their deepest values, hopes, dreams, and fears and that the activities noted above facilitate this expression. Additionally, he asserts that celebrations, festivals, and the like provide ways to affirm shared beliefs and values and create a sense of solidarity within a community.

Bates (1984) stresses that rituals and ceremonies are more than special, scheduled events. Indeed, he asserts that educational routines are culturally potent rituals and that their impact needs to be recognized so that they can support ethical ends. Starratt (1991) concurs and specifically discusses routine and special rituals that support an ethic of care.

> Through reward procedures and ceremonies as well as through school emblems, school mottos, school songs, and other symbols, the school communicates what it cares about. When the school rewards academic competition in ways that pit students against each other, when the awards are few and go only to the top students in the formal academic disciplines, then the school makes a clear statement of what it values. Other ceremonies and awards that stress caring cooperation, service, teamwork, and the like send different messages. Some schools clearly promote a feeling of family and celebrate friendship, loyalty, and service. Laughter in the halls, frequent greetings of each other by name, symbols of congratulations for successful projects, frequent displays of student work, hallways containing pictures of groups of youngsters engaged in school activities, cartoons poking fun at teachers and administrators—these are all signs of a school environment that values people for who they are. When youngsters engage every day in such a school community, they learn the lessons of caring, respect, and service to each other. With some help from peers and teachers, they also learn how to forgive, mend a bruised relationship, accept criticism, and debate different points of view. (p. 197)

SUMMARY

Throughout this chapter, I have described possible and probable indicators that an educational administrator is, indeed, seeking to operate under an ethic of care. I have, thus, attempted to write a description—not a prescription—focusing on three general role expectations caring leaders would seek to fulfill. It is entirely possible that my words may have some prescriptive value, especially to educators who feel a commitment to personal and community development but are stymied as to ways they might manifest caring in their specific environment. Furthermore, it is not only possible, but quite probable, that there are many more ways this kind of school leadership might manifest itself. Indeed, because acts of caring are to some extent context specific, I anticipate that my future efforts to delve into this topic will uncover additional traits or activities consistent with this ethic. I suspect, in fact, that I will find that those seeking to facilitate their own growth and learning along with the development of students and teachers will find themselves discovering an infinite number of ways to fulfill the deepest and finest purposes of school leadership.

6 Preparation Programs for Caring Administrators

> Programs in educational administration must begin to identify themselves as major avenues for the moral and intellectual education of aspiring administrators. National, state, and other agencies concerned with the training and education of administrators should encourage such programs to develop and apply more consistent concepts dealing with moral, ethical, political, and equity issues in both coursework and program development. Such programs should be encouraged to investigate new and different paradigms for the training and education of administrators, concentrating on the idea of administrative science as a specifically moral science.
>
> (William Foster, "Educational Administration: A Critical Appraisal," 1988, in D. E. Griffiths, R. T. Stout, & P. B. Forsyth (Eds.), *Leaders for America's Schools,* p. 78)

In recent years, the critical need for competent, capable school leaders has appeared time and time again in reform literature (see Murphy, 1990c, 1991, for an overview). Embedded in this concept are three assumptions that have implications for colleges and universities engaging in administrator preparation. The first assumption is that, heretofore, preparation programs have generally failed to adequately prepare persons for effective leadership. The second is that reform is needed in these programs if substantial changes are to occur in our schools, and the third is that leadership—and by extension the schools being led—will improve if preparation efforts improve. (For examples and discussions of these assumptions, see, e.g., Foster, 1988; Griffiths, Stout, & Forsyth, 1988; Hawley, 1988; Immegart, 1989; Murphy, 1990a, 1990b; Peterson & Finn, 1988; and Pitner, 1988). In this chapter I accept these assumptions, emphasizing, like the scholars just cited, that preparation, although important, is only one of an array of factors capable of affecting practice. Building on the framework discussed thus far in this book, I offer some thoughts on components of a course of study for caring administrators.

Several features of the ethic and practice of care have influenced my proposals. Because this ethic would compel administrators to sort through numerous ideas and perspectives competing to influence them, a preparation program should have an epistemological dimension. Such an emphasis would assist leaders in recognizing the influences of various forces on their understanding of hypotheses, theories, research data, and the like (Foster, 1988; Scarr, 1985). Because a caring ethic is concerned with the genuine promotion of human welfare, administrators governed by it must possess the ability to understand persons and situations and the knowledge that will enable them to use this understanding to engage in compassionate and developmentally sound activities. An adequate course of study should focus on developing administrators' analytical abilities wherein they would develop skills in recognizing the many issues, questions, and possibilities embedded in complex situations (Hills, 1975). Caring's commitment to maximum personal growth would also require that administrators possess an understanding of human development and of the forces that influence this phenomenon (Kegan, 1982; Levine, 1987). Additionally, the social ecology emphasis of this ethic, with its assumption that the welfare of individuals and that of their communities are linked, would necessitate that caring school leaders understand the multiple contexts in which schools exist (Ashton & Webb, 1986; Bellah et al., 1985). Administrators holding this perspective would also recognize the importance of each part of the social ecosystem functioning in a healthy manner. Since schools are, by definition, pedagogical institutions, caring leaders would emphasize the instructional leadership dimensions of their role, and preparation programs would seek to assist them in this area (Evans, 1989, 1991a, 1991b; Murphy & Hallinger, 1987). Additionally, leaders committed to nurturing school communities would recognize that their management strategies can help or hinder the development of such organizations. Programs concerned with adequately preparing such leaders would, thus, have a managerial dimension (Hoy & Miskel, 1987). Because caring is an intensely practical activity, programs seeking to prepare ethical leaders would have experiential and ethical dimensions, dimensions that would ideally flavor all courses offered.

In the following section, I discuss each of these components, offering, to borrow from Swift, "modest proposal[s]" for courses of study for ethical school leadership. The discussion is ordered as follows. I begin by examining the epistemological dimension, for this, in my view, is a necessary starting point in that it would help administrators understand their personal and professional conceptions of constructs such as "knowledge," "truth," "facts," "beliefs," and "ethics," and it would aid them in understanding the views of others. I then discuss some possible ways to approach the analytical dimension of preparation, a dimension closely linked to the epistemological one, for the latter would focus on the "what" and "why" of administrative knowledge, and the former on "how" this knowledge might be applied. My focus shifts, next, to the developmental and sociocultural dimensions of an adequate and effective course of study.

These would be concerned with supplying administrators with an understanding of the context of schooling on both the micro-, individual level and the macro-, sociocultural level. The pedagogical and managerial dimensions then claim my attention as I examine ways training might help leaders fulfill these two important functions. Finally, I offer some thoughts about the experiential and ethical dimensions, suggesting ways that theories and concepts and actual practice might have a healthy, appropriate reciprocal influence.

In my examination of the first six, I follow the same general format, discussing general goals or objectives behind each dimension and ways courses might be structured to meet these goals. For the experiential and ethical dimensions, I take a slightly different approach, arguing that these cannot be isolated from other aspects of administrative life and work and, therefore, ideally should not be relegated to separate courses. Instead, ethics and issues of actual practice should interface with the content of every course in a training program. I suggest some ways this might be accomplished.

In this chapter, I do not directly discuss issues such as strategies for monitoring entrance into programs, ideal credentials for faculty members, and the like. My avoidance of these topics is, in part, due to the constraints of time. It also, though, reflects my view that standardized scores, degrees or titles, years of experience, and so on have, at best, only an oblique relationship to an administrator's ability to care for her/his school, faculty, and students. I would argue that caring, effective practice has a much stronger link with "will, intention, experience, and value" (T. B. Greenfield, 1988, p. 151) and that an ethically oriented preparation program can facilitate personal and professional maturity in these arenas.

EPISTEMOLOGICAL AND ANALYTICAL DIMENSIONS: LAYING A FOUNDATION

The Epistemological Dimension

Sandra Scarr (1985), in an illuminating article published in the *American Psychologist*, reminds scholars of the need to consider how and why they "know" as they do. She argues that "knowledge of all kinds, including scientific knowledge, is a construction of the human mind . . . [and that] we cannot perceive or process knowledge without the constraints of belief" (p. 499). In asserting this, Scarr in no way denigrates the importance of rigorously pursuing knowledge and using it to enhance the quality of life. Rather, she cautions against becoming so wedded to a view of reality that one forgets that the view involves interpretations, perceptions, and assumptions.

Scarr's words have important implications for those concerned with preparing caring educational administrators, for this ethic calls leaders to examine their fundamental ideas and beliefs about the nature of persons, the purposes of education, and the roles of leaders in achieving these purposes. Additionally, it places a high premium on understanding and respecting the views of others. Preparation programs committed to facilitating these activities would, therefore, emphasize epistemological understanding. Stressing that reality can be viewed through many lenses and that no single view permits a completely accurate and comprehensive perspective, these programs would include courses to help school leaders understand the cognitive, emotional, social, and cultural forces that influence the lenses they and others use. The following, because they are consistent with the emphases of a caring ethic and with the demands of a rigorous academic program, might be objectives of this programmatic component:

1. Students will be able to articulate their personal philosophy of educational leadership and to discuss various factors that have influenced the development of their views.
2. Students will demonstrate a knowledge of alternative philosophies and of the assumptions and beliefs undergirding these perspectives.
3. Students will be able to map the evolution of administrative thought and practice and to locate the development of this field within the larger context of epistemological trends in the physical and social sciences.
4. Students will be able to trace likely linkages between assumptions about knowledge, social and cultural experiences, moral and ethical beliefs, and educational practices.
5. Students will demonstrate a general understanding of the principles and assumptions underlying quantitative and qualitative research. Furthermore, they will be able to critically assess examples of both noting strengths and weaknesses in theoretical frameworks, data gathering and analysis strategies, and conclusions.

Ideally, courses exploring epistemological issues would be taken early in a student's academic career, for they would introduce perspectives capable of informing, energizing, and illuminating subsequent study. A brief analysis of each of these objectives reveals how this might occur. For example, fulfilling Objective 1, with its emphasis on students' analyzing and articulating personal and professional philosophies, would encourage reflection upon conscious and subconscious beliefs and values. This, in the view of Foster (1986a, 1986b, 1988, 1989), T. B. Greenfield (1988), Sergiovanni (1992), and Starratt (1991), is central to ethical and effective administration. They assert that "administrators are essentially value-carriers in organizations; they are both arbiters of values and representatives of them" (T. B. Greenfield, 1988, p. 147) and that ethical leaders will seek to embrace those values most conducive to personal and community well-being.

The focus on equipping students to understand alternative views (Objective 2) is also central to caring administrative practice. Indeed, at the heart of this ethic is a commitment to respect the views of others, a respect that necessarily entails knowing what those views are (Buber, 1958, 1965; Fromm, 1956; Mayeroff, 1971). Grasping the ways administrative thought has evolved and understanding forces that have influenced this evolution (Objective 3) would help educators gain an understanding of the ideological underpinnings of administrative and pedagogical theories and practices. Critical theorists, including Bates (1983), Foster (1986a, 1986b, 1988, 1989), and T. B. Greenfield (1988), and feminist scholars, including Shakeshaft (1987), Ferguson (1984), Schmuck (1987), and Noddings (1984, 1989), have been especially vocal in asserting that ethical school leaders must understand the ideological underside of existing strategies and structures, and of the many recommendations for changing these.

The fourth objective's emphasis on contemplating the links between knowledge, culture, ethics, and practice would begin to address an issue cited as a deficiency in many preparation programs—a lack of relevance to actual practice (e.g., Achilles, 1988; Peterson & Finn, 1988; Sergiovanni, 1984). Tracing the link between knowledge and practices should help students see that these four phenomena are, indeed, related and that competent, caring leadership practices occur within a context that includes individual and shared ideas, assumptions, interpretations, and beliefs (Beck, 1990; Dokecki, 1982; Hodgkinson, 1978, 1983). The final objective reflects a response to concerns—expressed by Clark and Astuto (1988), Griffiths and co-authors (1988), Immegart (1989), and Peterson and Finn (1988)—that most preparation programs have, at best, only a hazy sense of the place of research in the preparation of practitioners. A course of study that stressed the value of administrators assessing various investigation strategies would commit itself to the position that practitioners would probably benefit more from learning to think about and use research than from devoting time and energy to one highly circumscribed study. Such a perspective would be based on the belief that administrative practice is complex, involving the ability to draw upon many sources of information and to apply insights derived from these sources in contextually appropriate ways.

A number of approaches might be useful in meeting these epistemological objectives. Griffiths and co-authors (1988) call for courses dealing with "the theoretical study of educational administration" (p. 294). If approached in the manner recommended by these authors, such courses would provide an excellent foundation for a comprehensive preparatory experience. Reflecting on the words of Jelinke, Smiricich, and Hirsch (1983; see also Morgan, 1986), Griffiths and co-authors suggest that a course might focus on unpacking the multiple images associated with the school organization.

Another possible course might focus on the etiology and scholarly, practical, and ethical implications of the many paradigms currently in play in administrative circles. Such a course might even be team taught by professors and practitioners holding differing perspectives. Surely, discussions, debates, and disagreements between professional colleagues would reinforce that "there is *no* royal road to knowledge" (Dokecki, 1990, p. 165). It would also give students a direct view of the ways paradigms influence conclusions, preferred theories, and interpretations of experiences.

Hodgkinson (1978, 1983) and T. B. Greenfield (1988) suggest that studies of a philosophical nature should be featured in preparation programs. Hodgkinson (1978) argues that administration, by its very nature, deals with "formulation of purpose, . . . value-laden issues, and the human component of organization" (p. 5) and that philosophy is the discipline that delves most readily into these issues. Greenfield concurs, stating:

> The world of will, intention, experience, and value is the world of organizations and administration. The building of a new science of administration will depend on our ability to understand these realities. It will require that we recognize their complexity (Hodgkinson, 1983, pp. 57–91) and their personal and subjective dimensions (Greenfield, 1985). Such a science will require methods and instruments that are adequate to these realities. As Schumacher (1977, pp. 39–60) points out, the question of what constitutes adequate methods and instruments for understanding the world is essentially a philosophical one. (p. 151)

Ideally, a course in philosophy, if offered, would be taught by administrator-philosophers who could draw clear links between the world of ideas and the realm of practice.

Historical analysis of the evolution of administrative thought and practice might also assist school leaders in assessing forces influencing current epistemological assumptions and actions. Courses devoted to such an analysis could be structured in several ways. They could, for example, look at the development of expectations, assumptions, and actions associated with a specific role. Sweeping historical analyses could be supplemented by case studies that offer in-depth examinations of educational leadership in a specific setting. Historically oriented courses might also emphasize analyzing the social, cultural, scientific, and political events that apparently influenced educational administration.

The first four objectives might conceivably be achieved in one or two courses. In all likelihood, the last objective—equipping students to assess and interpret research—would need to be covered in a separate course or courses. For example, a two-course sequence, with the first focusing on an overview of research assumptions and strategies and the second comparing studies taking different approaches, might be useful. Both courses might revolve around student inquiry. In the first, teams could investigate and report on various investigative paradigms. In the second, they might read research reports on administrative issues, compare the various approaches, and report to other students on their work. Alternatively, they might develop problems or questions based on their experiences and design (and perhaps implement) studies to address these. Discussions during this process would offer students a first-hand opportunity to discover the possibilities and limitations of research. The combined impact of these courses would do much to prepare leaders to evaluate the many ideas, opinions, policies, cost–benefit studies, and research reports being thrown at them from various quarters.

The Analytical Dimension

In addition to cultivating an informed awareness of the assumptions and beliefs that undergird thought and action and inculcating in students basic knowledge of research strategies, a program concerned with preparing ethical leaders would stress applying these awarenesses to actual situations. This would require the development of the type of analytical skills described by Hills (1975).

> Although I'm very unsure about the means of doing it, a heavy emphasis needs to be placed on the development of analytical skills. I do not mean skill in the application of analytical-conceptual schemes, but skills in "taking apart" issues, situations, and problems; dividing complex questions, operations, and situations into manageable parts; "looking across" cases for similarities and differences. (p. 13)

The objectives of courses aimed at cultivating students' analytical abilities might include the following:

1. Students will demonstrate their ability to observe objectively and describe—in detail—educational situations.
2. They will further demonstrate their ability to systematically "dissect" situations and to offer rationales for analytical strategies and evidence to support conclusions.
3. Additionally, they will formulate appropriate administrative actions based on these analyses. These actions should reveal an awareness of practical constraints (i.e., staff members' abilities, budgetary limitations); personal, professional, social, and cultural concerns; and ethical assumptions and commitments.

Courses aimed at accomplishing these objectives, like those concerned with epistemology, ideally would be taken early in a program of study. These two emphases would complement each other, with one stressing analyses of ways of knowing and the other focusing on in-depth analyses of actual and possible ways of acting. Like Hills, Sergiovanni (1984) stresses the importance of these objectives in the preparation of caring administrators. Asserting that "educational administration is a science of designing courses of action aimed at changing existing conditions" (p. 278), Sergiovanni argues that school leaders must be able to accurately describe and analyze situations if they are to devise strategies for transforming these situations. His words provide a nice explication of the ways that careful observations and thoughtful analyses lay a foundation for ethical practice.

> Of interest are accurate and reliable descriptions of the real world and how it works. With respect to administrative and organizational behavior, for example, relationships would be explained, linked together, and predicted. Laws and rules which govern behavior would be sought. . . . No progress can be made in developing a theory of practice if the themes of prediction and explanation, the hallmarks of traditional scientific inquiry, are not included. In a theory of practice, however, the ledger is incomplete without the normative side of science or the "ought" side. (p. 280)

Sergiovanni underscores the reality that making ethical decisions that genuinely influence practice requires astute analysis of "the concrete facts which exist in a situation" (p. 285). By extension, a preparation program concerned with moral leadership must, therefore, cultivate administrators' analytical skills.

Again, several approaches might be helpful in this area. Schön's (1987) discussion of educating for reflective practice suggests one of these. He writes of the value of "reflective conversation[s]" (p. 78) between experienced and novice practitioners. In his view, the experienced persons possess a "repertoire of examples, images, understandings, and actions" built on "past experience" (p. 66), which enable them to engage in an analytical dialogue with the novice in which "similarities and differences" (p. 67) between past and current experiences are articulated and possible courses of action are discussed. In the context of a class, students might pair up and engage in reflective conversations about case studies, actual situations reported in newspapers or magazines, or personal situations in which they are or have been involved. This type of course could be taken at virtually any point during the preparation program. If, however, it was taken by students early in their training, it could arm them with analytical skills and with a larger repertoire of experiences (drawn from the conversations) to use in future courses. Additional benefits of this approach would be the building of friendships between students and the development of their dialogical skills. Both of these could contribute to the ability of students to function as caring leaders in their various positions.

Brieshke (1990), Farquhar (1970), Greene (1991), Jackson (1988), Popper

(1990), and Witherell and Noddings (1991) suggest another strategy for developing analytical skills. They note that narratives—presented as novels, short stories, and historical accounts—can provide cases for analysis and discussion. Popper presents an articulate rationale for this approach. He argues that stories, told without the customary constraints imposed on "official" case studies (i.e., anonymity and limitations in the number of perspectives revealed), can permit administrators to plumb the depths of situations. Jackson, writing specifically about the incorporation of "a black perspective" in training programs, agrees. She states:

> The black perspective calls for a greater emphasis on the arts and humanities. Such an emphasis would be profitable for all potential administrators, for is not a truly liberated person one who has developed an appreciation for the human spirit in all its dimensions? Can we perhaps learn more about human nature and the way people act and react by reading the creative works of our novelists, poets, and play writers? (p. 313)

Still another analytical approach is suggested by the writings of Bolman and Deal (1984, 1991). Noting that the perspectives a person holds influence her or his interpretation of a situation, these authors suggest that leaders need to view situations through multiple "frames," described as "windows on the world, and lenses that bring the world into focus" (1991, p. 11). Bolman and Deal discuss four—the structural frame, the human resource frame, the political frame, and the symbolic frame—and offer helpful examples of the ways viewing a situation through each of these adds to knowledge and understanding. A class concerned with improving analytical skills might find it useful to discuss these perspectives and to carefully analyze situations from various "vantage points" (p. 11).

In addition to understanding situations as they are, transformative leaders would also seek to thoughtfully analyze what they might become under a variety of conditions, policies, programs, or problem solutions. A course that focused specifically on developing these projection skills, that allowed administrators to ask "what if" and to play out possible or likely scenarios, would, therefore, be entirely appropriate for school leaders. Such a course might focus on issues, principles, and patterns associated with carrying out of policies or decisions. Furthermore, it might encourage students to make and discuss "implementation estimates" (Allison, 1980, p. 241) wherein they seek to determine the cost of pursuing various plans or strategies. In a program concerned with effective and ethical school leadership, students would be encouraged to go beyond a mere cost–benefits type of estimate and to also consider nonquantifiable concerns such as moral imperatives and constraints and the impact of actions on personal and community well-being.

DEVELOPMENTAL AND SOCIOCULTURAL DIMENSIONS: UNDERSTANDING LARGER CONTEXTS

The Developmental Dimension

As noted throughout this book, a caring ethic is grounded in the idea that ethical actions are those which encourage healthy, holistic development of persons within the context of supportive, interdependent communities. Caring school officers must understand the dynamics of human development and both contextual and general characteristics and needs of communities. Programs to prepare such leaders must, therefore, promote the acquisition of developmental knowledge. They should also equip students to understand the larger social and cultural contexts in which this development occurs and to contemplate ways schools might promote the well-being of students, teachers, and their larger communities.

The developmental sequence might undertake to fulfill the following objectives:

1. Students will be able to outline major child development theories such as those of Erikson, Piaget, and Kohlberg and to discuss scholarly criticisms of these theories.
2. Using these theories, students will analyze and explicate specific classroom situations, exploring how student behavior fits within the various developmental frameworks and offering recommendations of appropriate educator behavior.
3. Students will also demonstrate knowledge of theories of adult development such as those offered by Erikson (1968, 1978), Levinson (1978), Kohlberg (1976), Sheehy (1977), and others. Additionally, they will critically assess various strategies for promoting personal and professional development within organizations [e.g., those offered by Argyris (1962, 1964), McGregor (1960), and Ouchi (1981)].
4. Combining the theories of professional and organizational growth with those dealing with adult development, students will analyze situations in which administrators deal with faculty and staff members, and will suggest effective and caring ways to conduct these interactions.

The importance of the first two objectives is emphasized by David Elkind (1981, 1984, 1987), who writes of a range of negative consequences in the lives of children when adults push children to develop too rapidly. In his view, this pushing deprives young people of the opportunity to pass through various growth stages in a natural and unhurried manner.

Hurrying children, expecting them to feel, think, and act much older than they are, stresses children. It puts extraordinary pressures upon them for adaptation. The consequences of hurrying are the usual symptoms of stress: headaches and stomachaches in preschoolers; learning problems and depression in elementary school children; and the whole gamut of teenage drug abuse, pregnancy, eating disorders, and suicide. Whatever the problems stemming from his or her individual life history, the hurried young person is clearly responding as much to external pressures as to internal conflicts. (1987, pp. xii–xiii)

He argues that educators, along with parents, must understand the patterns of development and safeguard the rights of children to move through these patterns at an appropriate pace.

W. Greenfield (1988), Griffiths and co-authors (1988), and Sergiovanni (1988) are among those who emphasize the importance of the third and fourth objectives, which stress promoting staff members' personal and professional growth. Greenfield's words express the need for administrative interpersonal skills grounded in the knowledge that preparation programs can provide. He writes:

To be interpersonally competent as a school administrator, one needs certain skills as well as a great deal of knowledge about teachers, the teaching task, and teachers' views of themselves, their students, and their work. A substantial formal knowledge base exists for all these areas (Wittrock, 1986), and much could be done . . . to introduce individuals to this knowledge and to provide them with opportunities to practice using that knowledge and the related interpersonal skills. (p. 224)

Ideally, these four objectives would be addressed in at least two courses, one dealing with implications of developmental theories for child-related administrative issues, and another focusing on supporting the personal and professional growth of faculty and staff. The emphasis in both of these courses would be on the ways school leaders might use these theories in executing the tasks associated with their roles to promote optimum development for young people and adults.

The first course might stress the acquisition and application of various developmental theories. This would require exposure to the seminal works in this area, an exposure that could be accomplished via a general developmental text or a seminar approach in which groups of students were responsible for discussing various theories. Students should also understand alternatives to some widely held views (see, e.g., Gilligan, 1982). The application component of this course might involve analyzing cases—drawn from texts, actual experience, or videos—from a developmental perspective. Using their knowledge of growth patterns, students could devise and discuss developmentally sound administrative actions.

The second course, focusing on supporting the growth of adults in the school setting, would also need to stress acquiring and applying knowledge. Works elucidating the needs and perspectives of teachers (e.g., Ashton & Webb, 1986; Rosenholtz & Simpson, 1990; Lortie, 1975), especially when read in light of the ideas on general adult development (e.g., Erikson, 1978; Levinson, 1978; Sheehy, 1977), would certainly be appropriate here. Narratives such as those by Conroy (1972), Kidder (1989), and Rose (1989) could also be helpful. Students might also be encouraged to tell their own stories, something that might be facilitated by encouraging them to keep a journal for a period of time (Witherell & Noddings, 1991).

In addition to learning about the needs and perspectives of colleagues, students would need to explore ways they, as administrators, might respond to these needs. Responses would involve definite actions, decisions, or policies (see, e.g., Ashton & Webb, 1986; Campbell, Cunningham, Nystrand, & Usdan, 1985), which could certainly be discussed in class settings. They would also, though, require that administrators communicate clearly with faculty and staff and that they demonstrate personal and professional support and respect. This would, therefore, be an appropriate place to focus on the development of skills in communication, problem solving, and negotiation (W. Greenfield, 1988; Hills, 1975; Sergiovanni, 1988). The approach in this course would, in all likelihood, differ from that used in many workshops and seminars in that the emphasis would be on building skills on a firm knowledge base (W. Greenfield, 1988). This represents an approach to the development of competence especially suited to preparation programs offered in colleges and universities, for these institutions have the personnel to emphasize the theories undergirding recommended actions (March, 1974).

The Sociocultural Dimension

The continuous growth and development of students and teachers are realities of the context in which administrators work. Another is the fact that schools exist within social systems. Administrators must contend with numerous extra-educational forces that affect their work (Campbell et al., 1987). Leaders guided by an ethic of caring would need to understand the many "forces outside school organizations that make a difference to school organizations" (p. 146) and to discover ways to work with these forces in order to promote a healthy social ecology, one that supports both individual and community development. The following objectives might be appropriate for a course(s) in this area:

1. Students will be able to identify major social and cultural trends influencing American education. They will also demonstrate a detailed knowledge of social and cultural forces affecting their own schools and school systems.
2. Additionally, they will demonstrate knowledge of official and unofficial systems by which various groups exert their influence on schools.
3. Students will also demonstrate their ability to use several approaches to understand the beliefs, meanings, assumptions, and expectations of various educational stakeholders.
4. They will develop a repertoire of administrative responses to extra-educational forces. These responses should reflect respect for persons represented by these forces and a commitment to work for individual and community development.

The importance of these objectives is stressed by Ashton and Webb (1986), who argue that teachers and, by extension, students and the school organization are affected by multiple environmental forces and that administrators must understand and work with these forces. Numerous articles in Golubchick and Persky's *Urban, Social, and Educational Issues* (1988) also underscore the powerful influence of culture on schools and the need for educators to respond knowledgeably and ethically to these influences. The perspective of the contributors to that volume is in line with the ecological and developmental emphases of a caring ethic. The unpacking of various social and cultural issues as done by Brofenbrenner (1988), Hodgkinson (1988), and others, combined with the implicit belief that schools should nurture holistic development of all persons, emphasizes the importance of administrators recognizing, respecting, and seeking to learn about the larger milieu.

Clearly, training programs, limited by time and faculty expertise, cannot focus on all of these. They can and should, however, identify those forces with the greatest potential to affect education and should emphasize ethical responses to these. Beck and Murphy (1993) identify three of these that seem "likely to have the most profound effect on education in the next century: . . . the perceived crisis in the economy, the changing nature of the social fabric of society, and the evolution from an industrial to a post-industrial world" (p. 179). Programs that assist administrators in dealing with these should have a dual emphasis. They must certainly provide students with "facts" about these trends. If, however, they stop at "just the facts," they will fall short of offering adequate preparation. Preparation programs must also assist prospective school leaders in understanding the interpretations and meanings various stakeholders attach to these and other facts.

Providing educators with the facts concerning actual and projected social and cultural trends might be accomplished, rather handily, by acquainting them with resources that can supply them with updated demographic information and with knowledge about local, state, and national systems for governing schools. Indeed, knowing where to look for statistics, budgets, laws, and policies is likely to be of much greater benefit to administrators than memorizing facts that are likely to become outdated. It might be helpful to involve reference librarians, school board members, local and state policy makers, attorneys, representatives of teachers' unions, professional associations, and various special interest groups, perhaps by inviting them to speak to classes. Alternatively, students could be responsible for investigating and reporting on information resources.

Facilitating an understanding of beliefs, meanings, interpretations, and expectations provides a much more interesting challenge to departments of educational administration. One approach might involve a comparative study of various cultures represented in schools. Students might explore the experiences and perceptions of African-Americans, Latinos, Asians, and others by reading fictional and nonfictional works or by conducting ethnographic studies. If representatives of any or all of these groups are involved in preparation programs, their participation in dialogues, discussions, or debates on sociocultural issues and education would be both appropriate and useful.

Another approach might be to study the tenets of various belief systems and ideologies, with special emphasis on their implications for education. Capitalism, socialism, communism, feminism, and religious fundamentalism are among those which might be examined. Students could explore the history of these views, read samples of work done by leaders in each, delve into the ethical systems each would hold, discuss each ideology's views on education, and formulate possible administrative responses.

Ashton and Webb's (1986) analysis of cultural forces affecting teachers suggests yet another way a course in this area might be structured. They note that educators work within at least four environments, which they label the "micro-, . . . meso-, exo-, and macrosystems" (p. 167). The first involves the classroom and the student–teacher interactions that occur therein. Ashton and Webb write that the mesosystem consists of two major environments that, separately and together, influence administrator–teacher–student interactions. These are the school, as a whole, and the home, where the work of teachers can be supported or impeded by parents. The exosystem is the policy-making environment, especially on the local and state levels, and the macrosystem is the larger society whose "cultural values . . . permeate our society [and] contribute to the social-psychological milieu that affects teachers' sense of efficacy" (p. 173). These two authors examine the impact of each of these systems on teachers and offer recommendations about possible changes on each level. A course might follow their general pattern. Taking issues such as multicultural education, reduced budgets and increased demands, accountability, teacher unions, and standardized curricula and tests, students might explore these four environments, attempting to discover their actual and potential impacts on education and formulating recommendations for actions that would result in healthier, developmentally sound systems.

PEDAGOGICAL AND MANAGERIAL DIMENSIONS: DEVELOPING SKILLS AND TECHNIQUES

Caring administration requires empathetic understanding and the commitment to act in supportive, nurturing ways. It also requires the mastery of technical skills. Indeed, caring and competence go hand in hand when it comes to educational leadership, and preparation programs must seek to cultivate both. The courses discussed thus far generally have stressed the cognitive side of administration, focusing on increasing leaders' knowledge bases and facilitating their abilities to think, to analyze, to reason, and to understand. A program must also help their students learn ways to act in order to promote optimal development. Two areas especially worthy of attention in this regard are pedagogical and managerial competence.

The Pedagogical Dimension

Recently, the idea of administrators, especially principals, functioning as instructional leaders has received a great deal of attention (see, e.g., Bossert, Dwyer, Rowan, & Lee, 1981; Duke, 1987; Murphy & Hallinger, 1987; Snyder, 1983). Interestingly, many who call upon administrators to become involved in the instructional arena feel that effective management is the key to success in this arena (see, e.g., Duke, 1987; Griffiths et al., 1988). Although management and pedagogy are certainly linked, they are not the same. Programs seeking to prepare caring school leaders will recognize this distinction and will seek to restore to educational leadership an emphasis on teaching (Evans, 1989, 1991a, 1991b).

Courses to contribute in this area might take the following as general objectives:

1. Students will evidence a knowledge of the learning process that goes beyond a kind of "black box" approach. That is, they will show that they understand not only that certain strategies are likely to produce certain outcomes, but also possible reasons for these outcomes.
2. When presented with various situations, they will be able to demonstrate their ability to recognize normal and variant student learning pat-

terns and to formulate and implement a range of pedagogical strategies to deal with individual differences in this area.

3. Students will also offer evidence of an understanding of seminal research focusing on the links between teachers' perceptions, their actions in classrooms, and student outcomes.
4. Again, presented with cases, they will also be able to demonstrate their ability to formatively evaluate teachers, and in simulations discuss their observations and recommendations in a supportive manner.

Evans (1989, 1991a, 1991b) offers a discussion of the importance of the first two objectives. He suggests that educational administration is, by its very nature, a pedagogical endeavor and that recognizing it as such is both logical and ethical.

> If the notion of administration or leadership (either one) is to be at all a meaningful notion, it must be a notion of leadership or administration that is rooted in a concern for the deep meaning and purpose of education, including its aims and intentions, as well as its hopes, its wishes and its dreams. In other words, it is the notion of *education* that gives the idea of leadership its whole purpose, rationality, coherence, intelligibility, meaningfulness, and so forth. (1991b, p. 3)

In the same vein, Sergiovanni (1988), citing Goodlad (1978, 1983) and Boyer (1983), argues that administration requires mastery of managerial, social, and pedagogical skills. "Technical, human, and educational forces of leadership, brought together in an effort to promote and maintain quality schooling, provide the critical mass needed for basic . . . competence" (p. 55).

Case studies of caring communities of learning further support the importance of administrators—at least on the school level—seeking to use their interactions with students to further educational purposes. Descriptions by Barth (1990), Grant (1988), Maeroff (1990), and Epstein (1990) all contain references to principals, assistant principals, and other administrators who sought to make time for direct contact with students and who used this time as an opportunity for a teaching–learning interaction.

The importance of the last two objectives, which involve administrators supporting and facilitating the work of teachers, has been noted quite often in recent administrative literature. The research of Armor and co-authors (1976), Ashton and Webb (1986), and Berman, McLaughlin, Bass, Pauly, and Zellman (1977), for example, underscores the links between student achievement, teachers' abilities, and teachers' sense of efficacy. And Barth (1990), Duke (1987), Snyder (1983), and numerous others write of ways administrators—via professional development activities and supportive personal interactions—can influence these variables by increasing actual and perceived effectiveness.

A course for administrators on "learning" might be one way to achieve the first and second objectives. A possible approach might revolve around the topic of cognitive development. Students could look at theories of learning through various stages of the life cycle (e.g., Kegan, 1982; Piaget, 1948, 1952, 1954) and consider normal and abnormal patterns of learning and implications of these for teaching strategies. Different members of the class might take an age, grade level, or developmental stage and develop a range of approaches to instruction, discipline, and organization that administrators could consider. Videos, debates, simulations, and role playing might all be used to develop skills in evaluating and implementing these strategies.

Evans's (1989, 1991a, 1991b) research methodology suggests yet another approach to improving administrators' pedagogical insight. He engages in a "strong reading" (1991b, p. 7) of nine principals' stories of practice, an activity described with the following words:

> To be engaged in the practice of doing a strong reading is, therefore, to be engaged in judging, in rendering a verdict. It is, as Gadamer (1975) suggests, a question of deciding what belongs to a practice, which is also and at the same time a question of deciding what does not belong. (1991b, p. 7)

For Evans, strong readings involve descriptively and normatively interpreting principals' actions in regard to their pedagogic activities. A preparation program might include a course that could afford students the opportunity to engage in such readings, using case studies, journal entries, and other descriptions of administrative work.

Professors seeking to address objectives three and four might also consider several possible approaches. Classes open to administrators and teachers could provide opportunities for dialogues and discussions that would allow members of both groups to better understand the needs, concerns, and perspectives of others. These discussions could be sparked by actual experiences of students or by case studies, videos, or even fictional accounts. Discussions of research on the links between administrators, teachers, and students (e.g., Rosenholtz & Simpson, 1990) might also be good resources.

Another approach might first stress research on the links between teacher perceptions, their classroom strategies, and student outcomes. Attention might then shift to ways administrators might work with teachers who are using less than effective approaches in their classes. Role playing, simulations, videos, and panel discussions with administrators and teachers could facilitate increased awareness on the part of both groups and improved communication and problem-solving skills.

Yet another approach might organize around key variables linked to teaching and learning. These could include curriculum and program development, accountability issues, evaluation and supervision strategies, organizational approaches to facilitate learning, various governance strategies, and so forth. Certainly these topics could not be covered in their entirety in one or two administrative courses. They could, however, be examined as they relate to a single administrative issue (e.g., middle school leadership, teacher empowerment, multicultural or urban education, or school leadership and shrinking budgets).

Still another course in this phase of the program might focus on a relatively unexamined area in educational administration—working with "at-risk" (Young, 1989–1990, p. 35) or ineffective teachers. One component of this course might concentrate on identifying persons "with a high potential for success in teaching" (Young, 1989–1990, p. 35). Students could evaluate the research (e.g., Bruno, 1991; Grissmer & Kirby, 1987; Hawley, 1986; Holland, 1985; Meek, 1988; Pigge, 1985; Pratt, 1986; Young, 1989–1990) on this topic. They could also reflect on their personal experiences and observations. A second component might deal with improving administrators' evaluative strategies. Duke's (1987) and Sergiovanni and Starratt's (1988) works provide insights on various strategies and offer cases for analysis. Videos of actual classroom situations might also be used. In the final section of this course, students could turn their attention to promoting instructional effectiveness. Professional development strategies (see, e.g., Barth, 1988, 1990) and communication and problem-solving skills (see, e.g., Keirsey & Bates, 1978; Sergiovanni & Starratt, 1988) could be discussed and practiced in simulated school situations.

The Managerial Dimension

In addition to being competent pedagogues, administrators of schools that are caring communities must be good managers. Indeed, one might view the possession of skills in this area as a necessary, but not sufficient, condition for effective and ethical leadership. Preparation programs should, therefore, include courses emphasizing the development of skill in this arena. Objectives might include the following:

1. Students will understand basic principles of financial management and planning in schools, and they will demonstrate their ability to use these principles in actual situations.
2. They will be able to demonstrate their understanding of basic concepts and uses of information processing systems by developing an ideal system for a real or hypothetical situation.
3. Additionally, students will explore time management strategies, discussing options that might free administrators to focus on caring, personal interactions.

4. They will also evidence a general understanding of major legal issues affecting school operation.

Griffiths and co-authors (1988) are among those who note the importance of these objectives. These authors choose the phrase "technical core" to describe the managerial skills—some related to pedagogy; others to "running a school"—needed by administrators. They write:

> Every profession has a core of technical knowledge that its practitioners must possess. Educational administration is no different. It too has a core of technical knowledge with which the administrators must be familiar (note we did not say master or be expert in). Most superintendents and principals will have staff people who are experts in the various aspects of the technical core. The superintendent and principal need to know enough of the technical core to be able to direct and monitor the work of others who are, presumably, experts. March (1974) in this Cocking Lecture of 1973, discusses in considerable detail the management of expertise. Having an understanding of the technical core is one aspect of that ability. (p. 295)

Peterson and Finn (1988) agree that the knowledge and skills base of administrators should extend the management strategies. Citing recommendations by the American Association of School Administrators (1982), they state that one area of expertise should be "'instructional management systems' and how to run them" (p. 100). Mackett, Frank, Abrams, and Nowakowski (1988) concur, especially stressing that administrators should possess expertise in the use of computers.

> Computer use bears directly on the effectiveness of the entire educational enterprise. Computers are not only extending and enriching the learning experience and creating new options for instructional and service delivery (Bork, 1987; Kinzer, Sherwood, and Bransford, 1986). They are also putting in the hands of education administrators more sophisticated and powerful tools for managing the education process (Bruno, 1986; Caffarella, 1985; Frank, Mackett, Abrams, and Nowakowski, 1986). (p. 234)

Zirkel and MacMurtrie (1988) discuss the importance of the last objective. Noting that most educators know little of legal decisions that affect their work, they offer a compendium of recent "education-related decisions of the Supreme Court and other such sources of law" (p. 18). Campbell and co-authors' (1987) overview of influences on administration also underscores the importance of leaders' being aware of legal mandates and constraints, for they note that various laws and policies have had an important effect on schools during the past half-century.

Griffiths and co-authors (1988) suggest that aspiring administrators might find it beneficial to take courses in other departments, especially in schools of business, to increase their skills in managing finances and information systems. Such a recommendation certainly has merit, but it also has a number of potential pitfalls. School administrators, in courses designed for MBAs, CPAs, economists, and financial planners, are likely to find themselves wading through material with little direct relevance to educational leadership. A better solution might be using as adjunct faculty, school business managers, practicing superintendents and principals, and others actually involved in management. The insights, problems, and techniques introduced by these practitioners could be supplemented, if needed, by readings or lectures offering conceptual perspectives. Indeed, giving students an opportunity to assess the relevance of management theories in light of stories of actual practice could prove quite valuable. Students could also explore management techniques in a course devoted solely to the analysis of cases. They might develop strategies to cope with various problems or concerns and assess their potential to be effective and ethical.

Another approach is suggested by Campbell and co-authors' *The Organization and Control of American Schools* (1985). In a systematic manner these authors look at administrative issues at each level of educational governance. Additionally, they explore issues such as special interest and minority groups, limited resources, the influence of colleges and universities, and the interplay between public and private education, which affect the work of leaders on all levels. The format used by these authors could be specifically adapted to a course on school management. Students could consider management strategies at different governance levels, with their varied resources, responsibilities, and spheres of control. Additionally, they might explore concerns caused by budgetary limitations, the demands of special interest groups, attempts of colleges and universities to influence schooling, and the like. This type of course would be especially valuable in programs where students worked or aspired to work in a range of administrative positions.

A basic skills approach might also be useful in this phase of the program. Different managerial competencies could be identified, and students could study, practice, and ultimately demonstrate abilities in these areas. The objectives noted at the beginning of this section—focusing on the management of money, time, personnel, and technology, within limits set by law or policy—represent areas that could be studied. Duke (1987) also writes of competencies recommended by the American Association of School Administrators (discussed in Hoyle, 1985) and Lipham (1982). He then discusses his conceptions of needed skills summarized on the "Duke Instructional Improvement Checklist" (p. 299). Such a list might provide a guide for a course component aimed at increasing managerial competence.

EXPERIENTIAL AND ETHICAL DIMENSIONS:
APPLYING SKILLS AND KNOWLEDGE

Two themes seem to dominate criticisms of current administrator preparation programs. The first is that much training has little relevance for actual practice. The second theme is that school leaders and the programs training them have, generally, ignored questions of ethics or values (Foster, 1988; Greenfield, 1991; Murphy, 1992).

Various suggestions to address these criticisms have been offered. The possibility of administrative students engaging in a "long-term internship" (Foster, 1988, p. 79) or an "apprenticeship" (Achilles, 1988, p. 51), for example, has been acclaimed as a way to link theory and practice. Griffiths and co-authors (1988) offer a slight variation on this idea. Instead of a single practicum experience, they recommend "a series of short, special-purpose internships with a master administrator" (p. 297). William Greenfield (1988), focusing on the development of moral competency, calls for some type of "formal moral socialization efforts" (p. 223) to assist administrators in reasoning ethically and applying their thoughts to practice. Many programs have, in some way, attempted to implement these recommendations—frequently by instituting a required practicum and offering, as an elective, a course in ethics or moral philosophy.

I agree with the sentiments behind these programmatic developments. An appropriate goal for training programs should be the contributing to the development of persons capable of competent and ethical practice. I would argue, however, that instituting a mandatory course involving supervised practice (usually occurring at the end of coursework) and an optional course in ethics is not the best way to achieve such a goal. Instead, I would propose that both issues of practice and ethics should be woven into the entire fabric of the preparatory experience. If students desire or need a clinical experience, then it should surely be offered. It is illogical and unnecessary, though, to require persons already working full-time in schools (as is the case with most educational administration students; see, e.g., Peterson & Finn, 1988; Griffiths et al., 1988) to take leaves from their work in order to "practice" their skills. In the same vein, courses devoted to ethics may be both useful and appropriate. Faculty should be careful, though, not to imply that ethical leadership is treated as something separable from other dimensions of administration (or that they are separable from one another) when, in fact, it is not. Ethical practice is the heart of school leadership and should be a focus in every course offered.

This might be accomplished in a number of ways. As noted in earlier discussions, analyses of case studies have the potential to play a central role in the preparation of school leaders. Participants in a program who are simultanously working in schools could supply cases from their own experiences. Ideally, these would reflect actual, ongoing problems with which the student, the school, its current administrators and teachers, or the district is grappling. The substance of the cases could vary depending on students' particular situations and the particular topic being emphasized. If, for example, students were focusing on developing managerial skills, cases could involve management problems. If instructional leadership was being emphasized, cases, similarly, could deal with this topic. As an alternative (or in addition) to topically oriented cases, students could be asked, early in the preparation program, to identify a major concern or problem facing them or their schools and to write a detailed description of this as a "case." This description would include an exploration of the structural and political dimensions of the situation. It should also include a discussion of ethical and personal concerns—both the student's and those of other involved parties. As they move through the program, students could be asked to use insights gained to analyze and develop ethically sound and effective strategies for dealing with their cases. If possible and appropriate, they could also be encouraged to implement these strategies and assess the intended and unintended outcomes.

Using cases provided by students that reflect their needs, concerns, and problems has several advantages. First, it would, in all likelihood, embue the material being studied with meaning. As they link concepts, theories, and reports of research to actual situations, students should be better able to see relationships and applications of abstract ideas. Second, it should enhance the ability of prospective school leaders to think critically about educational scholarship. As they seek to use and apply concepts, they will find that some are of greater usefulness than others. With faculty and other students, they should be encouraged to think through this phenomenon, exploring the limitations and contributions of theory and recommendations based on research. Third, faculty members working collaboratively with students on cases would shift the model of learning in preparation programs away from a traditional academic one, where the faculty are considered to be learned experts, and practitioners, ignorant novices, to a more collaborative, practice-oriented model. Professors would be unable to pick cases supporting their pet theories, cases where they had the solutions "figured out." Rather, they would have the opportunity continually to discover ways knowledge could be applied in order to improve schools and solve problems. As they took advantage of this opportunity, they would learn with and from students. Not only would this keep persons in the academic world up-to-date with issues of practice, but it would also symbolically bear witness to the fact that practitioners and practical knowledge are on a par with professors and researchers and with knowledge emanating from universities and research centers. It would demonstrate the value of *all* aspects of educational scholarship and practice. Finally, if students and faculty worked together on actual cases, there exists the possibility that they might be able make real, relatively immediate contributions to school improvement. If this leads to even a few strategies that help to solve pressing problems of practice, such an effort would be worth-while.

Using cases from practice, in a sense, involves bringing issues of practice into administrator preparation programs. Another option for linking experience and ethics with practice might be providing students and faculty with the opportunity to engage in various forms of service in educational settings *while* they are taking courses. Students working in schools could be encouraged to take on some task beyond their usual job description. Those not in schools could spend several hours a week providing, developing, and/or working in some sort of service effort benefitting students, teachers, parents, administrators, or others. These experiences could provide a grounding and a focus for productive academic endeavors and for caring and effective administrative practice in the future.

In regard to their impact on coursework, these service opportunities could provide cases for analysis. Unlike the case studies discussed in the preceding paragraphs, those generated from the type of opportunities I have described would probably lead students into unfamiliar areas. For in their service, students would go beyond their usual professional activities and engage in something extra—something that meets an educational need and relates to a student's interest or concern—which, without the encouragement of a structured assignment, they would not, in all likelihood, be able to do. For the prospective administrator, encounters with the unfamiliar, which they could discuss and analyze with colleagues in the program, would be of great value. For according to most accounts, the practice of educational leadership is riddled (or blessed) with situations that demand quick action and almost immediate response. The kind of experience I am describing would provide students with a chance to transition into this reality. They would be encountering situations of actual practice, which allow little time for thought or reflection, but their time in preparation programs would allow students to withdraw a bit from these to reflect on events, their responses, and the reasons and meanings underlying both.

Engaging in service activities as a part of their preparation could also encourage future leaders to grapple with questions regarding personal and professional ethical commitments and values. Being in a position where they were seeking to respond to some educational need would certainly enable these individuals to gain deeper insight into the complex circumstances that breed needs. Particularly for those who have had little personal experience with poverty, discrimination, and the like, these opportunities should give them a chance to examine their own assumptions about the links between merit and opportunity, quality and equality, and achievements and external circumstances. Additionally, if the observations of Barbour (1992), De Pree (1989), and Greenleaf (1977) have any merit, participation in service would provide invaluable experience for those seeking to lead in a caring manner. Indeed, De Pree asserts that an ideal administrator is one who "leads through serving" (p. 119), and Greenleaf links the metaphor of servant to the notion of leadership, suggesting that one can be successful in the latter only if she or he is also the former. Arguing that education can and should equip persons to live together in societies characterized by interdependence and mutual respect and service, Barbour suggests that preparation for professional and personal life should include opportunities to serve and to think and learn about the meanings and values attached to such an activity.

On a practical level, the benefits of either approach described above might be maximized in several ways. The possibility of students keeping journals was briefly discussed earlier in this chapter. This would certainly be one strategy for encouraging them to draw connections between experience, ethics, and academics. In these, they could reflect on their studies, their work, and links between the two. They could report on thoughts and feelings as they encounter various situations. Additionally, they could chronicle problem-solving processes, engage in inner debates, celebrate success, examine failures, and describe possible or desirable scenarios (see Cooper, 1991, for an in-depth discussion of journal writing). Students could discuss various entries with other students or professors or use them to write papers that require linking theory and practice.

Another approach might involve faculty members interacting with students in ways that take them beyond the weekly class session. Regularly meeting in small groups would allow for discussions of pressing issues and concerns. These interactions could serve the functions of cultivating supportive relationships, of allowing persons to vicariously experience situations through listening to others' narratives, of encouraging the sharing of successful strategies, and of enlisting the wisdom of others in problem-solving situations. Special seminars or workshops might also be held throughout the academic year where persons from various walks of life could discuss specific topics related to caring and effective administrative practice. These could deal, in some detail, with issues relevant to different types of administrators. For example, those in schools where unions are a strong force might benefit from attending sessions on ethically and effectively working with these organizations. Administrators in urban schools might focus on issues related to school leadership in those settings, and those leading schools characterized by diversity, poverty, high percentages of students from broken homes or dysfunctional families, shrinking budgets, large numbers of handicapped children, a high level of teacher turnover, or student problems with drugs, premature sexual activity, violence, gangs, eating disorders, and such, might appreciate the opportunity to examine, in detail, issues of special concern.

Programs might also emphasize issues of ethical, knowledgeable practice by creating a final experience, assignment, or requirement stressing such concerns. Students might be asked to create a kind of portfolio in which they include personal cases and reports and reflections on their work in regard to pedagogy, management, school culture, faculty development, and the like. Additionally, they might write a paper on one or several cases in which they demonstrate theoretical knowledge, analytical skills, ethical awareness, instructional leadership expertise, and managerial competence. Alternatively, the culminating assignment might involve a combination of written and oral work. Students could take a topic especially relevant to their work (e.g., disciplinary strategies in multicultural environments, school site professional development, team teaching and the principal, AIDS education strategies), become something of an "expert" on that topic, and develop a presentation for other students and professors.

FACULTY ATTITUDES: A CRITICAL FACTOR

It is doubtful that even the best planned programs can produce caring school leaders if the professors leading these courses fail to act in supportive ways toward students and colleagues. Several forces often mitigate against these kinds of interactions, one of the most notable being the great myth of academia that caring, collegial relationships and research, publications, tenure, and promotions cannot co-exist. Professors of educational administration, guided by the ethic of caring, must work to explode this myth. They must endeavor to find a balance between their own scholarship and their interactions with others. In their scholarship, they must pursue excellence, and in their interactions, kindness and mutual support. For some, this task may seem easy; for others, it may appear to be formidable. Regardless, it is inescapable for academicians who are genuinely concerned with developing caring and competent school leaders consistent with an ethic of care.

Concluding Thoughts

We must love one another or die.
(W. H. Auden, September 1, 1939, in *The Oxford Dictionary of Quotations*, 1979, p. 20)

In the course of writing this book, I have discussed my ideas with professors, other graduate students, and practicing administrators and teachers. Not infrequently, when I mention that I am studying the ethic of caring in educational administration, I receive slightly cynical responses.

—"There are no ethics in administration";
—"Caring and educational administration—what a 'nice' idea"; or
—"Caring administrators—That's really an oxymoron."

These words suggest a certain frustration on the part of educators, frustration that pressures so often force them to ignore the personal and interpersonal dimensions of their work. I do not doubt that these pressures are real and fierce, but I would argue that, insofar as they deny opportunities to care and to be cared for, they are fundamentally anti-educational and need to be challenged, denied, or resisted.

The work of educators differs from that of professionals in other fields in its opportunity to influence the holistic growth of persons and their communities. Teachers and administrators, on a daily basis and over an extended period of time, work with young people as they pass through their formative years. They have the privilege of creating environments where persons can learn and develop as healthy, moral, responsible, competent spouses, parents, workers, citizens, friends, and individuals. *This is education.* Anything less or different represents a reductionistic, bastardized understanding of our field.

Educational leaders must embrace and celebrate the fact that their work is centered on persons and communities. They must accept the fact that this means that they lead "organizations [that] are a nexus of freedom and compulsion, . . . [where] conflict is endemic" (T. B. Greenfield, 1988, p. 151). In these organizations, control is limited, results are unpredictable, and choices are often "paradoxical" (Clark & Astuto, 1988, p. 112), with no course of action clearly good or bad, right or wrong. Administrators uncomfortable with these realities might do well to seek jobs outside of education, for their attempts to squeeze schools into the images of factories, corporations, military organizations, or laboratories and to run them accordingly cannot and will not ultimately succeed. Those who choose education must, instead, seek leadership strategies uniquely suited to schools. Such strategies must include a consideration of caring ways to promote personal and community growth. These strategies may be difficult to implement; their results may be difficult to measure; their goals may at times be unattainable. They must, however, be sought. The alternative—a system of schools where persons' values depend on what they do, not on who they are; where right actions are judged in terms of the ability to produce the best workers at the lowest costs; and where the complexity and wonder of human life is ignored in order to develop neat workable systems—is unthinkable.

References

Abbott, M. G., & Caracheo, F. (1988). Power, authority, and bureaucracy. In N. Boyan (Ed.), *Handbook of research on educational administration* (pp. 239–257). New York: Longman.

Achilles, C. (1988). Unlocking some mysteries of administration and administrator preparation: A reflective prospect. In D. E. Griffiths, R. T. Stout, and P. B. Forsyth (Eds.), *Leaders for America's schools.* (pp. 41–67). Berkeley, CA: McCutchan.

Adler, M. J. (1982). *The Paideia proposal.* New York: Macmillan.

Aljose, S. A., & Joyner, V. G. (1990, Summer). Cooperative learning: The rebirth of an effective teaching strategy. *Educational Horizons,* 197–202.

Allison, G. T. (1980). Implementation analysis: The "missing chapter" in conventional analysis illustrated by a teaching exercise. In L. Lewin & E. Vedung (Eds.), *Politics as rational action: Essays in public choice and policy analysis* (pp. 237–260). Boston: D. Reidel.

American Association of Colleges of Teacher Education. (1988). *School leadership: A preface for action.* Washington, DC: Author.

American Association of School Administrators. (1985). *Raising standards in schools: Problems and solutions.* Arlington, VA: Author.

Angus, L. (1988, April). *School leadership and educational reform.* Paper presented at the annual meeting of the American Educational Research Association, New Orleans.

Arendt, H. (1978). *The life of the mind: Thinking.* New York: Harcourt Brace Jovanovich.

Argyris, C. (1957). *Personality and organization.* New York: Harper & Row.

Argyris, C. (1962). *Interpersonal competence and organizational effectiveness.* Homewood, IL: Irwin-Dorsey.

Argyris, C. (1964). *Integrating the individual and the organization.* New York: Wiley.

Armor, D., Conry-Osequera, P., Cox, M., King, N., McDonnell, L., Pascal, A., Pauly, E., & Zellman, G. (1976). *Analysis of the School Preferred Reading Program in selected Los Angeles minority schools.* Santa Monica, CA: The Rand Corporation.

Ashton, P. T., & Webb, R. B. (1986). *Making a difference: Teachers' sense of efficacy and student achievement.* New York: Longman.

Bacharach, S. B., & Conley, S. C. (1989). Uncertainty and decisionmaking in teaching: Implications for managing line professionals. In T. J. Sergiovanni & J. H. Moore (Eds.), *Schooling for tomorrow: Directing reforms to issues that count* (pp. 311–329). Boston: Allyn & Bacon.

Bane, M. J. (1989). Children and the welfare state: The changing role of families. In
    L. H. Golubchick & B. Persky (Eds.), *Urban, social, and educational issues* (pp.
    296–300). Garden City, NY: Avery.

Barbour, B. (1992). *An aristocracy of everyone: The politics of education and the future
    of America.* New York: Ballantine.

Barth, R. S. (1988). School: A community of learners. In A. Lieberman (Ed.), *Building
    a professional culture in schools* (pp. 129–147). New York: Teachers College Press.

Barth, R. S. (1990). *Improving schools from within: Teachers, parents, and principals
    can make the difference.* San Francisco: Jossey-Bass.

Bates, R. J. (1983). *Educational administration and the management of knowledge* (ESA
    Monograph 891). Victoria, Australia: Deakin University Press.

Bates, R. J. (1984). Toward a critical practice of educational administration. In T. J. Ser-
    giovanni & J. E. Corbally (Eds.), *Leadership and organizational culture: New per-
    spectives on administrative theory and practice* (pp. 260–279). Urbana: University
    of Illinois Press.

Beane, J. A. (1990, Winter). Affective dimensions of effective middle schools. *Educa-
    tional Horizons,* 109–112.

Beare, H. (1989, September). *Educational administration in the 1990s.* Paper presented
    at the national conference of the Australian Council for Educational Administra-
    tion, University of New England, Armidale, New South Wales, Australia.

Beck, L. G. (1990). *Conceptual frameworks for understanding individual–group inter-
    action.* Unpublished manuscript, Vanderbilt University, Nashville.

Beck, L. G., & Marshall, C. (1992). Policy in practice: A qualitative inquiry into the work
    of sexuality educators. *Educational Policy, 6*(3), 319–334.

Beck, L. G., & Murphy, J. (1993). *Understanding the principalship: Metaphorical
    themes, 1920s–1990s.* New York: Teachers College Press.

Beck, L. G., & Newman, R. (1992, October). *Caring in contexts of diversity: Notes from
    the field.* Paper presented at the annual meeting of the University Council for Edu-
    cational Administration, Minneapolis.

Becker, H. J. (1990). Curriculum and instruction in middle-grade schools. *Phi Delta
    Kappan, 71*(6), 450–458.

Bellah, R. N., Madsen, R., Sullivan, W. M., Swidler, A., & Tipton, S. M. (1985). *Habits
    of the heart: Individualism and commitment in American life.* New York:
    Harper & Row.

Bennis, W. G. (1984). Transformative power and leadership. In T. J. Sergiovanni & J. E.
    Corbally (Eds.), *Leadership and organizational culture: New perspectives on ad-
    ministrative theory and practice* (pp. 72–84). Urbana: University of Illinois Press.

Berliner, D. C. (1976). Impediments to the study of teacher effectiveness. *Journal of
    Teacher Education, 27,* 5–13.

Berman, P., McLaughlin, M., Bass, G., Pauly, E., & Zellman, G. (1977). *Federal pro-
    grams supporting educational change: Factors affecting implementation and con-
    tinuation.* Santa Monica, CA: The Rand Corporation.

Berry, B., & Ginsberg, R. (1990). Effective schools, teachers, and principals: Today's
    evidence, tomorrow's prospects. In B. Mitchell & L. Cunningham (Eds.), *Educa-
    tional leadership and changing contexts of families, communities, and schools:
    Eighty-ninth yearbook of the National Society for the Study of Education* (pp. 155–
    183). Chicago: University of Chicago Press.

Blackham, J. H. (1959). *Six existentialist thinkers.* New York: Harper & Row.

Blau, P. M., & Scott, W. R. (1962). *Formal organizations: A comparative approach.* San Francisco: Chandler.

Bloom, A. (1987). *The closing of the American mind.* New York: Simon & Schuster.

Blustein, J. (1991). *Care and commitment: Taking the personal point of view.* Oxford: Oxford University Press.

Bolman, L. G., & Deal, T. E. (1984). *Modern approaches to understanding and managing organizations.* San Francisco: Jossey-Bass.

Bolman, L. G., & Deal, T. E. (1991). *Reframing organizations: Artistry, choice, and leadership.* San Francisco: Jossey-Bass.

Bork, A. (1987). *Learning with personal computers.* New York: Harper and Row.

Bossert, S. T., Dwyer, D. C., Rowan, B., & Lee, G. V. (1981). *The instructional management role of the principal: A preliminary review and conceptualization.* San Francisco: Far West Laboratory for Educational Research and Development.

Bowlby, J. (1952). *Maternal care and mental health* (2nd ed.). Geneva: World Health Organization.

Bowlby, J. (1958). The nature of a child's tie to its mother. *International Journal of Psychoanalysis, 39,* 350–373.

Bowlby, J. (1969). *Attachment and loss:* Vol. 1. *Attachment.* New York: Basic.

Bowlby, J. (1973). *Attachment and loss:* Vol. 2. *Separation.* New York: Basic.

Boyd, W. L. (1987). Public education's last hurrah? Schizophrenia, amnesia, and ignorance in school politics. *Educational Evaluation and Policy Analysis, 9*(2), 85–100.

Boyer, E. L. (1983). *High school: A report on secondary education in America.* New York: Harper & Row.

Brabeck, M. M. (Ed.). (1989). *Who cares? Theory, research, and educational implications of the ethic of care.* New York: Praeger.

Brann, E. T. (1979). *Paradoxes of education in a republic.* Chicago: University of Chicago Press.

Bredeson, P. V. (1985). An analysis of the metaphorical perspectives of school principals. *Educational Administration Quarterly, 21*(1), 29–50.

Bredeson, P. V. (1987). Language of leadership: Metaphor making in educational administration. *Administrators Notebook, 32*(6), 1–5.

Bredeson, P. V. (1988). Perspectives on schools: Metaphors and management in education. *The Journal of Education, 26*(3), 293–310.

Bridges, E. (1988). Coping with incompetent teachers. In L. H. Golubchick & B. Persky (Eds.), *Urban, social, and educational issues* (pp. 156–161). Garden City, NY: Avery.

Brieshke, P. A. (1990). The administrator in fiction: Using the novel to teach educational administration. *Educational Administration Quarterly, 26*(4), 376–393.

Brieshke, P. A. (1991, April). *Interpreting ourselves: Administrators in modern fiction.* Paper presented at the annual meeting of the American Educational Research Association, Chicago.

Brinelow, P. (1985). Competition for public schools. In B. Gross & R. Gross (Eds.), *The great school debate: Which way for American education?* (pp. 345–353). New York: Simon & Schuster.

Brofenbrenner, U. (1978). Who needs parent education? *Teachers College Record, 79,* 773–774.

Brofenbrenner, U. (1988). Alienation and the four worlds of childhood. In L. H. Golub-chick & B. Persky (Eds.), *Urban, social, and educational issues* (pp. 52–58). Garden City, NY: Avery.

Bruner, J. (1986). *Actual minds, possible worlds*. Cambridge, MA: Harvard University Press.

Bruno, J. E. (1986). *Designing educational systems using d Base II and the Apple II.* Palo Alto, CA: Blackwell Scientific Publications.

Bruno, J. E. (1991). *Re-examination of the role of assessment in promoting student learning.* Unpublished manuscript.

Bryk, A. (1988). Musings on the moral life of schools. *American Journal of Education,* 96(2), 256–290.

Buber, M. (1958). *I and thou* (2nd ed.; R. G. Smith, Trans.). New York: Charles Scribner's Sons.

Buber, M. (1965). *Between man and man.* New York: Macmillan.

Buchmann, M. (1989). The careful vision: How practical is contemplation in teaching? *American Journal of Education,* 98(1), 35–61.

Burlingame, M. (1984). Theory into practice: Educational administration and the cultural perspective. In T. J. Sergiovanni & J. E. Corbally (Eds.), *Leadership and organizational culture: New perspectives on administrative theory and practice* (pp. 295–305). Urbana: University of Illinois Press.

Button, H. W. (1966). Doctrines of administration: A brief history. *Educational Administration Quarterly,* 2(3), 216–224.

Caffarella, E. P. (1985). *Spreadsheets go to school: An administrator's guide to spreadsheets.* Reston, VA: Reston.

Callahan, R. E. (1962). *Education and the cult of efficiency.* Chicago: University of Chicago Press.

Campbell, R. F., Cunningham, L., Nystrand, R. G., & Usdan, M. (1985). *The organization and control of American schools* (5th ed.). Columbus, OH: Merrill.

Campbell, R. F., Fleming, T., Newell, L. J., & Bennion, J. W. (1987). *A history of thought and practice in educational administration.* New York: Teachers College Press.

Carnegie Council on Adolescent Development. (1989). *Turning points.* Washington, DC: Author.

Carnegie Forum on Education and the Economy. (1986). *The nation prepared: Teachers for the 21st century.* New York: Carnegie Forum.

Centers for Disease Control. (1988). Guidelines for effective school health education to prevent the spread of AIDS. *Morbidity and Mortality Weekly Report, 37,* S-2.

Chapman, D., & Lowther, M. (1982). Teachers' satisfaction with teaching. *Journal of Educational Research, 75,* 241–247.

Chase-Lansdale, L., Dempsey, V., Noblitt, G. W., & Rogers, D. (1991, April). *Coming to care in the context of classrooms.* Symposium presentation at the annual meeting of the American Educational Research Association, Chicago.

Chilman, C. (Ed.). (1983). *Adolescent sexuality in a changing American society.* New York: Wiley.

Chubb, J. E. (1988). Why the current wave of school reform will fail. *The Public Interest, 90,* 28–49.

Clark, D. L., & Astuto, T. (1988). Paradoxical choice options in organizations. In D.

Griffiths, R. Stout, & P. Forsyth (Eds.), *Leaders for America's schools* (pp. 112–130). Berkeley, CA: McCutchan.

Clark, D. L., & Meloy, J. M. (1989). Renouncing bureaucracy: A democratic structure for leadership in schools. In T. J. Sergiovanni & J. H. Moore (Eds.), *Schooling for tomorrow: Directing reforms to issues that count* (pp. 272–294). Boston: Allyn & Bacon.

Clegg, S. (1981). Organization and control. *Administrative Science Quarterly, 26,* 545–562.

Coegan, P. N., & Raebeck, B. S. (1989, December). Cooperation, integration, and caring in public education. *NASSP Bulletin,* pp. 96–100.

Cohen, A. (1990). *Caring kids: Altruism and empathy.* Paper presented at the annual meeting of the National Association of Independent Schools, Washington, DC.

Cohen, D. K. (1976). Loss as a theme in social policy. *Harvard Educational Review, 46,* 553–571.

Cohen, M., & March, J. G. (1974). *Leadership and ambiguity.* New York: McGraw-Hill.

Compton, N., Duncan, M., & Hruska, J. (1987). *How schools can help combat student pregnancy.* Washington, DC: National Education Association.

Conley, S. C. (1989, March). *Who's on first? School reform, teacher participation, and the decision-making process.* Paper presented at the annual meeting of the American Educational Research Association, San Francisco.

Conroy, P. (1972). *The water is wide.* New York: Bantam.

Cooper, J. E. (1991). Telling our own stories: The reading and writings of journals or diaries. In C. Witherell & N. Noddings (Eds.), *Stories lives tell: Narrative and dialogue in education* (pp. 96–112). New York: Teachers College Press.

Corcoran, T. B. (1989). Restructuring education: A new vision at Hope Essential High School. In J. M. Roswow & R. Zager (Eds.), *Allies in educational reform.* San Francisco: Jossey-Bass.

Council for Chief State School Officers. (1988). A concern about AIDS and adolescents. *Concerns,* pp. 1–8.

Council for Chief State School Officers. (1989). *Success for all in a new century.* Washington, DC: Author.

Cox, H. (1965). *The feast of fools: A theological essay on festivity and fantasy.* Cambridge, MA: Harvard University Press.

Crowson, R. L., & Porter-Gehrie, C. (1980). The discretionary behavior of school principals in large city schools. *Educational Administration Quarterly, 16*(1), 45–69.

Cuban, L. (1976). *Urban school chiefs under fire.* Chicago: University of Chicago Press.

Cuban, L. (1984). *How teachers taught.* New York: Longman.

Cuban, L. (1988). *The managerial imperative and the practice of leadership in schools.* Albany: State University of New York Press.

Curwin, R. L., & Mendler, A. N. (1989). *Discipline with dignity.* Alexandria, VA: Association for Supervision and Curriculum Development.

Cusick, P. A. (1983). *The egalitarian ideal and the American high school: Studies of three schools.* New York: Longman.

Darling-Hammond, L. (1985). Mad-hatter tests of good teaching. In B. Gross & R. Gross (Eds.), *The great school debate: Which way for American education?* (pp. 247–251). New York: Simon & Schuster.

Darling-Hammond, L. (1988). Accountability and teacher professionalism. *American Educator, 12*(4), 8–13.

David, J. (1989). *Restructuring in progress: Lessons from pioneering districts.* Washington, DC: National Governors' Association.

Davidson, N. (1989). Small group cooperative learning in mathematics: A review of research. In N. Davidson & R. L. Dees (Eds.), *Research in small group cooperative learning in mathematics.* Reston, VA: National Council of Teachers of Mathematics.

Deal, T. E., & Peterson, K. (1990). *The principal's role in shaping school culture.* Washington, DC: General Printing Office.

DeCharms, R. (1972). Personal causation training in the schools. *Journal of Applied Psychology, 2*(2), 95–113.

Deci, E. (1971). Effects of externally mediated rewards on intrinsic motivation. *Journal of Personality and Social Psychology, 18,* 105–115.

Delderfield, R. F. (1972). *To serve them all my days.* New York: Washington Square Press.

De Pree, M. (1989). *Leadership in art.* New York: Doubleday.

Dewey, J. (1959). *Moral principles in education.* New York: Philosophical Library.

Dillon, D. R. (1989). Showing them that I want them to learn and that I care about who they are: A microethnography of the social organization of a secondary low-track English-reading classroom. *American Educational Research Journal, 26*(2), 227–259.

Dodd, P. (1965). *Role conflicts of school principals.* Washington, DC: U.S. Department of Health, Education, and Welfare.

Dokecki, P. R. (1982). Liberation: Movement in theology, theme in community psychology. *Journal of Community Psychology, 10,* 185–196.

Dokecki, P. R. (1987a). Can knowledge contribute to the creation of community? *Journal of Community Psychology, 15,* 90–96.

Dokecki, P. R. (1987b). History and policy: A necessary connection. *Religious Education, 82*(3), 360–374.

Dokecki, P. R. (1990). On knowing the person as agent in caring relations. *Person-Centered Review, 5*(2), 155–169.

Duke, D. L. (1987). *School leadership and instructional improvement.* New York: Random House.

Dunlap, D. M., & Goldman, P. (1991). Rethinking power in schools. *Educational Administration Quarterly, 27*(1), 5–29.

Elder, S. (1990). The power of the parent. In *Yale Magazine.* New Haven, CT: Yale University.

Eliot, T. S. (1971). *The complete poems and plays, 1909–1950.* New York: Harcourt, Brace, & World.

Elkind, D. (1981). *The hurried child: Growing up too fast too soon.* Reading, MA: Addison-Wesley.

Elkind, D. (1984). *All grown up and no place to go: Teenagers in crisis.* Reading, MA: Addison-Wesley.

Elkind, D. (1987). *Miseducation: Preschoolers at risk.* New York: Alfred A. Knopf.

Ellett, C. D., & Masters, J. A. (1978, August). *Learning environment perceptions:*

Teacher and student relations. Invited paper presented at the American Psychological Association, Toronto.

Ellul, J. (1964). *The technological society.* New York: Vintage.

Ellul, J. (1988). *Jesus and Marx: From gospel to ideology* (J. M. Hanks, Trans.). Grand Rapids, MI: William B. Eerdmans.

Elmore, R. F. (1988). Choice in public education. In W. L. Boyd & C. T. Kercher (Eds.), *The politics of excellence and choice in education.* New York: Falmer.

Elshtain, J. B. (1988). Reflections on child abuse. In L. H. Golubchick & B. Persky (Eds.), *Urban, social, and educational issues* (pp. 94–99). Garden City, NY: Avery.

Epstein, J. L. (1990). What matters in the middle grades—grade span or practices. *Phi Delta Kappan, 71*(6), 438–444.

Erdberg, C. B. (1988). Major issues in education. In L. H. Golubchick & B. Persky (Eds.), *Urban, social, and educational issues* (pp. 13–16). Garden City, NY: Avery.

Erikson, E. (1968). *Identity: Youth and crisis.* New York: W. W. Norton.

Erikson, E. (1978). *Adulthood.* New York: W. W. Norton.

Etzioni, A. (1960). *A comparative analysis of complex organizations.* New York: Free Press.

Eugene, T. (1989). Sometimes I feel like a motherless child. The call and response for a liberational ethic of care by black feminists. In M. Brabeck (Ed.), *Who cares? Theory, research, and educational implications of the ethic of care* (pp. 45–62). New York: Praeger.

Evans, D. L. (1990, October). The mythology of the marketplace in school choice. *Education Week,* p. 32.

Evans, P. R. (1989). *Ministrative insight: Educational administration as pedagogic practice.* Unpublished doctoral dissertation, University of Calgary.

Evans, P. R. (1991a, April). *Abstract of ministrative insight: Educational administration as pedagogic practice.* Paper presented at the annual meeting of the American Educational Research Association, Chicago.

Evans, P. R. (1991b, April). *Ministrative insight: Educational administration as pedagogic practice.* Paper presented at the annual meeting of the American Educational Research Association, Chicago.

Farquhar, R. H. (1970). *The humanities in preparing educational administrators* (State-of-the-knowledge Series, No. 7). University of Oregon: The ERIC Clearinghouse on Educational Administration.

Fay, B. (1975). *Social theory and political practice.* London: George Allen Unwin.

Fayol, H. (1949). *General and industrial management* (C. Stours, Trans.). London: Pitman. (Original work published 1919)

Feiman-Nemser, S., & Floden, R. E. (1986). The cultures of teaching. In M. Wittrock (Ed.), *Handbook of research on teaching* (pp. 505–526). New York: Macmillan.

Ferguson, K. E. (1984). *The feminist case against bureaucracy.* Philadelphia: Temple University Press.

Fine, M. (1992, October). *Democratizing choice: Reinventing public education.* Paper presented at the Economic Policy Institute Conference, Washington, DC.

Fine, R. (1985). *The meaning of love in human experience.* New York: John Wiley.

Finkelstein, B. (1984). Education and the retreat from democracy in the United States, 1979–1982. *Teachers College Record, 86,* 280–281.

Foster, W. P. (1984). Toward a critical theory of educational administration. In T. J. Sergiovanni & J. E. Corbally (Eds.), *Leadership and organizational culture: New perspectives on administrative theory and practice* (pp. 240–259). Urbana: University of Illinois Press.

Foster, W. P. (1986a). *Paradigms and promises: New approaches to educational administration.* Buffalo, NY: Prometheus.

Foster, W. P. (1986b). A critical perspective on administration and organization in education. In W. Foster & J. Oakes (Eds.), *Critical perspectives on the organization and improvement of schooling* (pp. 95–130). Boston: Kluwer Nijhoff.

Foster, W. P. (1988). Educational administration: A critical appraisal. In D. E. Griffiths, R. T. Stout, & P. B. Forsyth (Eds.), *Leaders for America's schools* (pp. 68–82). Berkeley, CA: McCutchan.

Foster, W. P. (1989, April). *School leaders as transformative intellectuals: A theoretical argument.* Paper presented at the annual meeting of the American Educational Research Association, San Francisco.

Fox, M. (1990). *A spirituality named compassion.* San Francisco: Harper.

Frank, F., Mackett, M., Abrams, P., & Nowakowski, J. (1986). The education utility and educational administration and management. In D. D. Gooler (Ed.), *The education utility: The power to revitalize education and society* (pp. 94–107). Englewood Cliffs, NJ: Educational Technology Publications.

Frankena, W. (1973). *Ethics* (2nd ed.). Englewood Cliffs, NJ: Prentice-Hall.

Freedman, S. G. (1990). *Small victories: The real world of a teacher, her students and their high school.* New York: Harper & Row.

Freire, P. (1970). *Pedagogy of the oppressed* (M. B. Ramus, Trans.). New York: Herder & Herder.

French, J. P. R., & Raven, B. H. (1959). The bases of social power. In D. Cartwright (Ed.), *Studies in social order* (pp. 150–167). Ann Arbor: University of Michigan Press.

Freud, S. (1926). *Collected papers* (Vol. 21). London: Hogarth.

Fromm, E. (1956). *The art of loving.* New York: Harper & Row.

Gadamer, H. G. (1975). *Truth and method.* New York: Seabury.

Gage, N. L. (1989). What do we know about teaching effectiveness? In L. H. Golubchick & B. Persky (Eds.), *Urban, social, and educational issues* (pp. 137–144). Garden City, NY: Avery.

Gaylin, W. (1976). *Caring.* New York: Knopf.

Gilligan, C. (1982). *In a different voice: Psychological theory and women's development.* Cambridge, MA: Harvard University Press.

Giroux, H. A. (1988a). *Schooling and the struggle for public life: Critical pedagogy in the modern age.* Minneapolis: University of Minnesota Press.

Giroux, H. A. (1988b). *Teachers as Intellectuals: Toward a critical pedagogy.* Granby, MA: Bergin & Garvey.

Giroux, H. A., & McLaren, P. (1988). Reproducing reproduction: The politics of tracking. In H. A. Giroux, *Teachers as intellectuals: Toward a critical pedagogy* (pp. 186–195). Granby, MA: Bergin & Garvey.

Giroux, H. A., Penna, A. N., & Pinar, W. F. (Eds.). (1981). *Curriculum and instruction: Alternatives in education.* Berkeley, CA: McCutchan.

Golubchick, L. H. (1989). The drug dilemma: Monster on the loose. In L. H. Golubchick & B. Persky (Eds.), *Urban, social, and educational issues* (pp. 305–308). Garden City, NY: Avery.

Golubchick, L. H., & Persky, B. (Eds.). (1988). *Urban, social, and educational issues.* Garden City, NY: Avery.

Goodlad, J. L. (1978). Educational leadership: Toward the third era. *Educational Leadership, 23*(4), 322–331.

Goodlad, J. L. (1983). *A study of schooling.* New York: McGraw-Hill.

Goodlad, J. L. (1984). *A place called school: Prospects for the future.* New York: McGraw-Hill.

Grant, C. (1988). *The world we created at Hamilton High.* Cambridge, MA: Harvard University Press.

Greene, M. (1991). Foreword. In C. Witherell & N. Noddings (Eds.), *Stories lives tell: Narrative and dialogue in education* (pp. ix–xi). New York: Teachers College Press.

Greenfield, T. B. (1985). *Putting meaning back into theory: The search for lost values and the disappeared individual.* Paper presented to the Annual Conference of the Canadian Society for the Study of Education, Montreal.

Greenfield, T. B. (1988). The decline and fall of science in educational administration. In D. E. Griffiths, R. T. Stout, & P. B. Forsyth (Eds.), *Leaders for America's schools* (pp. 131–159). Berkeley, CA: McCutchan.

Greenfield, T. B. (1991). Re-forming and re-valuing educational administration: Whence and when cometh the Phoenix. *Organizational Theory Dialogue.* Portland, OR: Portland State University, Organizational Theory Special Interest Group.

Greenfield, W. P. (Ed.). (1987). *Instructional leadership: Concepts, issues, and controversies.* Boston: Allyn & Bacon.

Greenfield, W. P. (1988). Moral imagination, interpersonal competence, and the work of school administrators. In D. E. Griffiths, R. T. Stout, & P. B. Forsyth (Eds.), *Leaders for America's schools* (pp. 207–233). Berkeley, CA: McCutchan.

Greenleaf, R. K. (1977). *Servant leadership.* New York: Paulist Press.

Griffin, R. (1990). An individualistic view. In individualism, community, and education: An exchange of views. *Educational Theory, 40*(1), 1–10.

Griffiths, D. E. (1988). *Educational administration: Reform PDQ or RIP* (Occasional paper no. 8312). Tempe, AZ: University Council for Educational Administration.

Griffiths, D. E., Stout, R. T., & Forsyth, P. B. (1988). The preparation of educational administrators. In D. E. Griffiths, R. T. Stout, & P. B. Forsyth (Eds.), *Leaders for America's schools* (pp. 284–304). Berkeley, CA: McCutchan.

Grissmer, D. W., & Kirby, S. N. (1987). *Teacher attrition: The uphill climb to staff the nation's schools.* Santa Monica, CA: The Rand Corporation.

Guthrie, J. W. (1990). The evolution of educational management: Eroding myths and emerging models. In B. Mitchell & L. Cunningham (Eds.), *Educational leadership and changing contexts of families, communities, and schools: Eighty-ninth yearbook of the National Society for the Study of Education* (pp. 210–231). Chicago: University of Chicago Press.

Habermas, J. (1984). *The theory of communicative action.* (Vol. 1). Boston: Beacon.

Habermas, J. (1988). *The theory of communicative action.* (Vol. 2). Boston: Beacon.

Halpin, A., & Croft, D. B. (1962). *The organizational climate of schools.* Washington, DC: U.S. Office of Education.

Harlow, H. F. (1958). The nature of love. *American Psychologist, 13,* 673–685.

Harlow, H. F. (1961). The maternal affectional system. In H. L. Rheingold (Ed.), *Maternal behavior in mammals*. New York: Wiley.

Hartrup, W. (1979). The social worlds of children. *American Psychologist, 34,* 944–950.

Hauerwas, S. (1981). *A community of character: Toward a constructive Christian social ethic.* Notre Dame: University of Notre Dame Press.

Hauerwas, S. (1983). *The peaceable kingdom: A primer in Christian ethics.* Notre Dame: University of Notre Dame Press.

Hawley, W. D. (1986). Toward a comprehensive strategy for addressing the teacher shortage. *Phi Delta Kappan, 67*(10), 712–718.

Hawley, W. D. (1988). Universities and the improvement of school management. In D. E. Griffiths, R. T. Stout, & P. B. Forsyth (Eds.), *Leaders for America's schools* (pp. 82–89). Berkeley, CA: McCutchan.

Higgins, A. (1989). The just community educational program: The development of moral role taking as the expression of justice and care. In M. M. Brabeck (Ed.), *Who cares? Theory, research, and educational implications of the ethic of care* (pp. 197–215). New York: Praeger.

Hills, J. (1975). The preparation of administrators: Some observations from the "firing line." *Educational Administration Quarterly, 11*(3), 1–20.

Hirsch, P., & Andrews, J. A. Y. (1984). Administrators' response to performance and value challenges. In T. J. Sergiovanni & J. E. Corbally (Eds.), *Leadership and organizational culture: New perspectives on administrative theory and practice* (pp. 170–185). Urbana: University of Illinois Press.

Hobbes, T. (1839). *The English works of Thomas Hobbes* (Vols. 1 & 2; W. Molesworth, Ed.). London: J. Bohn.

Hobbs, N., Dokecki, P. R., Hoover-Dempsey, K. V., Moroney, R. M., Shayne, M. W., & Weeks, K. H. (1984). *Strengthening families.* San Francisco: Jossey-Bass.

Hodgkinson, C. (1978). *Towards a philosophy of administration.* Oxford: Basil Blackwell.

Hodgkinson, C. (1983). *The philosophy of leadership.* New York: St. Martin's Press.

Hodgkinson, C. (1991). *Educational leadership: The moral art.* Albany: State University of New York Press.

Hodgkinson, H. (1988). Preface. In L. H. Golubchick & B. Persky (Eds.), *Urban, social, and educational issues* (p. iii). Garden City, NY: Avery.

Holland, J. L. (1985). *Making vocational choices.* Englewood Cliffs, NJ: Prentice-Hall.

Holmes Group. (1986, April). *Tomorrow's teachers: A report of the Holmes Group.* East Lansing, MI: Author.

Hough, J. C. (1990). The university and the common good. Unpublished manuscript.

Houston, H. M. (1989, March). *Professional development for restructuring: Analyses and recommendations.* Paper presented at the annual meeting of the American Educational Research Association, San Francisco.

Hoy, W., & Miskel, C. (1987). *Educational administration: Theory, research, and practice* (3rd ed.). New York: Random House.

Hoyle, J. R. (1985). Programs in educational administration and the AASA preparation guidelines. *Educational Administration Quarterly, 21*(1), 71–93.

Immegart, G. L. (1989). What is truly missing in advanced preparation in educational administration? *Journal of Educational Administration, 28*(3), 5–13.

Immegart, G., & Burroughs, J. M. (Eds.). (1970). *Ethics and the school administrator.* Danville, IL: Interstate.

Imre, R. W. (1982). *Knowing and caring: Philosophical issues in social work.* New York: University Press of America.

Jackson, B. L. (1988). Education from a black perspective with implications for administrator preparation programs. In D. E. Griffiths, R. T. Stout, & P. B. Forsyth (Eds.), *Leaders for America's schools* (pp. 305–313). Berkeley, CA: McCutchan.

Jelinke, M., Smiricich, L., & Hirsch, P. (1983). Organizational culture. *Administrative Science Quarterly, 19*(3), 245.

Jencks, C. (1972). *Inequality: A reassessment of the effect of family and schooling in America.* New York: Basic.

Johnson, D. W., & Johnson, R. T. (1989). *Cooperation and competition: Theory and research.* Edina, MN: Interaction.

Johnson, D., Johnson, R., Holobee, E. J., & Roy, P. (1984). *Circles of learning: Cooperation in the classroom.* Alexandria, VA: Association for Supervision and Curriculum Development.

Johnson, S. K. (1987). How to rejuvenate ho-hum teachers. Paper presented at the annual convention of the National School Boards Association.

Joyce, B., Hersh, R., & McKibbon, M. (1983). *The structure of school improvement.* White Plains, NY: Longman.

Kanter, R. (1977). *Men and women of the corporation.* New York: Basic.

Kearnes, D. L. (1988a, April). An education recovery plan for America. *Phi Delta Kappan, 69*(8), 565–570.

Kearnes, D. L. (1988b, April). A business perspective on American schooling. *Education Week, 7*(30), 24, 32.

Kegan, R. (1982). *The evolving self: Problem and process in human development.* Cambridge, MA: Harvard University Press.

Keirsey, D., & Bates, M. (1978). *Please understand me* (3rd ed.). Del Mar, CA: Prometheus Nemesis Books.

Kelley, B. F., & Bredeson, P. V. (1987). *Principals as symbol managers: Measures of meaning in schools.* Paper presented at the annual meeting of the American Educational Research Association, Washington, DC.

Kelsey, M. T. (1981). *Caring: How we can love one another?* New York: Paulist Press.

Kemp, J. (1970). *Ethical naturalism: Hobbes & Hume.* London: Macmillan.

Keniston, K. (1965). *The uncommitted: Alienated youth in American society.* New York: H. Wolf.

Keniston, K. (1976, February 19). The 11-year olds of today are the computer terminals of tomorrow. *New York Times.*

Kidder, T. (1989). *Among school children.* Boston: Houghton Mifflin.

Kinzer, C. K., Sherwood, R. D., & Bransford, J. D. (1986). *Computer strategies for education: Foundations and content-area applications.* Columbus, OH: Merrill.

Kirkpatrick, F. G. (1986). *Community: A trinity of models.* Washington, DC: Georgetown University Press.

Kirst, M. W. (1989). Who should control the schools? Reassessing current policies. In T. J. Sergiovanni & J. H. Moore (Eds.). *Schooling for tomorrow: Directing reforms to issues that count* (pp. 62–88). Boston: Allyn & Bacon.

Kirst, M. W., McLaughlin, M., & Massell, P. (1990). Rethinking policy for children: Implications for educational administration. In B. Mitchell & L. Cunningham (Eds.), *Educational leadership and changing contexts of families, communities, and schools: Eighty-ninth yearbook of the National Society for the Study of Education* (pp. 69–90). Chicago: University of Chicago Press.

Koenigs, S. S., Fiedler, M. L., & DeCharms, R. (1977). Teacher beliefs, classroom interactions, and personal causation. *Journal of Applied Social Psychology, 7*(2), 95–114.

Kohlberg, L. (1966). A cognitive-developmental analysis of children's sex-role concepts and attitudes. In E. Maccoby (Ed.), *The development of sex differences.* Stanford, CA: Stanford University Press.

Kohlberg, L. (1969). Stage and sequence: The cognitive development approach to socialization. In D. A. Goslin (Ed.), *Handbook of socialization theory and research.* Chicago: Rand.

Kohlberg, L. (1976). *Collected papers on moral development and moral education.* Cambridge, MA: Center for Moral Education.

Kohut, S. (1990, Winter). A quality middle school: What makes the difference? *Educational Horizons, 48*(3), 107–108.

Lee, H. (1960). *To kill a mockingbird.* New York: Popular Library.

Leithwood, K. A., & Montgomery, D. J. (1982). The role of the elementary school principal in program improvement. *Review of Educational Research, 52*(3), 309–339.

LeShan, E. (1985). A message from an underachiever. In B. Gross & R. Gross (Eds.), *The great school debate: Which way for American education?* (pp. 243–246). New York: Simon & Schuster.

Levine, M. D. (1987). *Developmental variation and learning disorders.* Cambridge, MA: Educators Publishing Service.

Levinson, D. J. (1978). *The seasons of a man's life.* New York: Alfred A. Knopf.

Lewis, C. S. (1947). *The abolition of man: How education develops man's sense of morality.* New York: Macmillan.

Lightfoot, S. L. (1983). *The good high school: Portraits of character and culture.* New York: Basic.

Likert, R. (1961). *New patterns of management.* New York: McGraw-Hill.

Likert, R. (1967). *The human organization.* New York: McGraw-Hill.

Lipham, J. (1982). *Leadership for educational improvement.* Paper presented at the Northwest Regional Educational Laboratory.

Lipsitz, J. (1984). *Successful schools for young adolescents.* New Brunswick, NJ: Transaction.

Lipsky, M. (1969). *Toward a theory of street level bureaucracy.* Madison: University of Wisconsin Press.

Little, J. W. (1982). Norms of collegiality and experimentation: Workplace conditions of school success. *American Educational Research, 19,* 325–340.

Lortie, D. C. (1975). *School teacher: A sociological study.* Chicago: University of Chicago Press.

Louis, K. S. (1990, April). *Workplace conditions related to teacher satisfaction.* Presentation at the National Graduate Student Seminar sponsored by the University Council of Educational Administrators, Boston.

Louis, K. S. & Miles, M. (1992). *Reforming the urban high school.* New York: Teachers College Press.

Lovell, J. T., & Phelps, M. S. (1976). *Supervision in Tennessee: A study of perceptions of teachers, principals, and supervisors.* Nashville: Tennessee Association for Supervision and Curriculum Development.

Maccoby, M. (1988, November–December). A new model for leadership. *Research Technology Management, 31*(6), 53–54.

Machiavelli, N. (1952). *The prince* (L. Ricci, Trans.). New York: Mentor. (Original work published 1532)

MacIntyre, A. (1966). *A short history of ethics.* New York: Macmillan.

MacIntyre, A. (1981). *After virtue: A study in moral theory.* South Bend, IN: University of Notre Dame Press.

MacIver, J. M. (1990). Staffing decisions in the middle grades: Balancing quality instruction and teacher/student relations. *Phi Delta Kappan, 71*(6), 465–469.

Mackett, M., Frank, F., Abrams, P., & Nowakowski, J. (1988). Computers and education excellence: Policy implications for educational administration. In D. E. Griffiths, R. T. Stout, & P. B. Forsyth (Eds.), *Leaders for America's schools* (pp. 233–248). Berkeley, CA: McCutchan.

Macmurray, J. (1933). *Interpreting the universe.* London: Faber & Faber.

Macmurray, J. (1950). *Conditions of freedom.* London: Faber & Faber.

Macmurray, J. (1957). *The self as agent.* London: Faber.

Macmurray, J. (1961). *Persons in relation.* New York: Harper and Brothers.

Maeroff, G. J. (1990). Getting to know a good middle school: Shoreham-Wading River. *Phi Delta Kappan, 71*(7), 504–511.

March, J. G. (1974). Analytical skills and the university training of administrators. *Journal of Educational Administration, 1*(8), 30–54.

Maritain, J. (1947). *The person and the common good* (J. J. Fitzgerald, Trans.). South Bend, IN: University of Notre Dame Press.

Marshall, C., Mitchell, D., & Wirt, F. (1989). *Culture and education policy in the American states.* New York: Falmer.

Martin, D. T. (1990). A critique of the concept of work and education in the school reform reports. In C. M. Shea, E. Kahane, & P. Sola (Eds.), *The new servants of power: A critique of the 1980s school reform movement* (pp. 39–56). New York: Praeger.

Martin, J. R. (1989). Transforming moral education. In M. M. Brabeck (Ed.), *Who cares? Theory, research, and educational implications of the ethic of care* (pp. 183–196). New York: Praeger.

Maslow, A. (1970). *Motivation and personality* (2nd ed.). New York: Harper & Row.

Mayeroff, M. (1971). *On caring.* New York: Harper & Row.

McGregor, D. (1960). *The human side of enterprise.* New York: McGraw-Hill.

McPartland, J. M. (1990). Staffing decisions in middle grades. Balancing quality instruction and teacher/student relations. *Phi Delta Kappan, 71*(6), 465–469.

McWilliams, W. C. (1973). *The idea of fraternity in America.* Berkeley: University of California Press.

Mead, M. (1970). *Culture and commitment: A study of the generation gap.* New York: Doubleday.

Meek, A. (1988). On teaching as a profession. A conversation with Linda Darling-Hammond. *Educational Leadership, 46*(3), 11–17.

Meyer, J., & Cohen, E. (1971). *The impact of the open-space school upon teacher influence and autonomy: The effects of an organization innovation.* Stanford, CA: Stanford University Press. (Eric Document Reproduction Service No. EP 602 291)

Mitchell, B. (1990a). Loss, belonging, and becoming: Social policy themes for children and schools. In B. Mitchell & L. Cunningham (Eds.), *Educational leadership and changing contexts of families, communities, and schools: Eighty-ninth yearbook of the National Society for the Study of Education* (pp. 19–51). Chicago: University of Chicago Press.

Mitchell, B. (1990b). Children, youth, and restructured schools: Views from the field. In B. Mitchell & L. Cunningham (Eds.), *Educational leadership and changing contexts of families, communities, and schools: Eighty-ninth yearbook of the National Society for the Study of Education* (pp. 52–68). Chicago: University of Chicago Press.

Mitchell, B., & Cunningham, L. (Eds.). (1990). *Educational leadership and changing contexts of families, communities, and schools. Eighty-ninth yearbook of the National Society for the Study of Education.* Chicago: University of Chicago Press.

Morgan, G. (1986). *Images of an organization.* Beverly Hills, CA: Sage.

Morris, R. (1986). *Rethinking social welfare: Why care for the stranger?* New York: Longman.

Morris, V. C., Crowson, R. L., Porter-Gehrie, C., & Horowitz, E. (1983). *Principals in action: The reality of managing schools.* Columbus, OH: Charles E. Merrill.

Mortimer, K. R., & McConnell, T. R. (1978). *Sharing authority effectively.* San Francisco: Jossey-Bass.

Muggeridge, M. (1971). *Something beautiful for God: Mother Teresa of Calcutta.* Garden City, NY: Doubleday.

Murphy, J. (1988). Methodological measurement, and conceptual problems in the study of instructional leadership. *Educational Evaluation and Policy Analysis, 10,* 117–139.

Murphy, J. (1990a). Preparing school administrators for the twenty-first century: The reform agenda. In B. Mitchell & L. Cunningham (Eds.), *Educational leadership and changing contexts of families, communities, and schools: Eighty-ninth yearbook of the National Society for the Study of Education* (pp. 232–251). Chicago: University of Chicago Press.

Murphy, J. (1990b). The reform of school administration: Pressures and calls for change. In J. Murphy (Ed.), *The reform of American public education in the 1980s: Perspectives and cases.* Berkeley, CA: McCutchan.

Murphy, J. (1990c). The educational reform movement of the 1980s: A comprehensive analysis. In J. Murphy (Ed.), *The reform of American public education in the 1980s: Perspectives and cases.* Berkeley, CA: McCutchan.

Murphy, J. (1990d). School administration responds to pressures for change. In J. Murphy (Ed.), *The reform of American public education in the 1980s: Perspectives and cases.* Berkeley, CA: McCutchan.

Murphy, J. (Ed.). (1990e). *The reform of American public education in the 1980s: Perspectives and cases.* Berkeley, CA: McCutchan.

Murphy, J. (1991). *Restructuring schools: Capturing and assessing the phenomena*. New York: Teachers College Press.

Murphy, J. (1992). *The landscape of leadership preparation*. New York: Teachers College Press.

Murphy, J., & Hallinger, P. (Eds.). (1987). *Approaches to administrative training*. Albany: State University of New York Press.

Murphy, J., Hallinger, P., Lotto, L. S., & Miller, S. K. (1987). Barriers to implementing the instructional leadership role. *Canadian Administrator, 27*(3), 1–9.

Murphy, J., & Hart, A. W. (1988, October). Preparing principals to lead in restructured schools. Paper presented at the annual meeting of the University Council for Educational Administration, Cincinnati.

Nash, R. (1990). A communitarian view. In individualism, community, and education: An exchange of views. *Educational Theory, 40*(1), 10–18.

National Education Association. (1983). *Investing in America's future: The role of public education in economic growth and the American Defense Education Act*. Washington, DC: Author.

National Governors' Association. (1986). *Time for results: The governors' 1991 report on education*. Arlington, VA: Author.

National School Board Association. (1984). *A blueprint for educational excellence*. Washington, DC: Author.

National School Board Association. (1987). *AIDS and the American public schools*. Alexandria, VA: Author.

Niebuhr, H. R. (1956). *The purpose of the church and its ministry*. New York: Harper.

Nisbet, R. (1990). *The quest for community: A study in the ethics of order and freedom*. San Francisco: Institute for Contemporary Studies.

Noddings, N. (1984). *Caring: A feminine approach to ethics and moral education*. Berkeley: University of California Press.

Noddings, N. (1988). An ethic of caring and its implications for instructional arrangements. *American Journal of Education, 96*(2), 215–230.

Noddings, N. (1989). Educating moral people. In M. M. Brabeck (Ed.), *Who cares? Theory, research, and ethical implications of the ethic of care* (pp. 216–233). New York: Praeger.

Noddings, N. (1992). *The challenge to care in schools: Alternative approaches to education*. New York: Teachers College Press.

Oakes, J. (1985). *Keeping track: How schools structure inequality*. New Haven, CT: Yale University Press.

Oliver, D. W. (1976). *Education and community: A radical critique of innovative schooling*. Berkeley, CA: McCutchan.

Ouchi, W. G. (1981). *Theory Z*. New York: Avon Books.

Palmer, P. (1983). *To know as we are known: A spirituality of education*. San Francisco: Harper & Row.

Parr, S. R. (1982). *The moral of the story: Literature, values, and American education*. New York: Teachers College Press.

Parsons, T. (1951). *The social system*. New York: Free Press.

Patina, P. (1988). *Metaphor and the high school principalship*. Unpublished doctoral dissertation, Hofstra University, Hempstead, NY.

Paul, E., & Pipel, H. (1979). Teenage pregnancy: The law in 1979. *Family Planning Perspective, 11,* 197–200.

Peacocke, A. (1990, December). In the face of God. *Life, 13*(15), 47–78.

Perkins, J. (1976). *Let justice roll down.* Glendale, CA: Regal.

Perkins, J. (1982). *With justice for all.* Ventura, CA: Regal.

Perrin, S. (1987). Metaphorical revelations: A description of metaphor as the reciprocal engagement of abstract perspectives and concrete phenomena in experience. *Metaphor and Symbolic Activity, 2,* 251–280.

Perrow, C. (1986). *Complex organizations: A critical essay* (3rd ed.). New York: Random House.

Peters, T. J., & Waterman, R. H. (1982). *In search of excellence: Lessons from America's best run companies.* New York: Harper & Row.

Peterson, K. D., & Finn, C. F. (1988). Principals, superintendents, and administrator's art. In D. E. Griffiths, R. T. Stout, & P. B. Forsyth (Eds.), *Leaders for America's schools* (pp. 89–108). Berkeley, CA: McCutchan.

Piaget, J. (1948). *The moral judgment of the child.* New York: Free Press.

Piaget, J. (1952). *The origins of intelligence in children.* New York: International Universities Press.

Piaget, J. (1954). *The construction of reality in the child.* New York: Basic.

Pigge, F. L. (1985). Teacher education graduates: Comparisons of those who teach and do not teach. *Journal of Teacher Education, 36*(4), 27–28.

Pilat, M. (1991). *Policy in practice: Portraits of parenting adolescents and the service delivery system.* Unpublished doctoral dissertation, Vanderbilt University, Nashville, TN.

Pilpel, H., & Rockett, L. (1981). Sex education and the law. In L. Brown (Ed.), *Sex education in the eighties: The challenge of healthy sexual evolution* (pp. 19–31). New York: Plenum.

Pitner, N. J. (1988). School administrator preparation: The state of the art. In D. E. Griffiths, R. T. Stout, & P. B. Forsyth (Eds.), *Leaders for America's schools* (pp. 367–402). Berkeley, CA: McCutchan.

Popper, S. H. (1990). *Pathways to the humanities in school administration* (3rd ed.). Tempe, AZ: University Council for Educational Administration.

Powell, A., Cohen, D. K., & Farrar, E. (1985). *The shopping mall high school: Winners and losers in the educational marketplace.* Boston: Houghton Mifflin.

Pratt, D. (1986). Predicting career success in teaching. *Action in Teacher Education, 8*(4), 25–34.

Psyzkowski, I. S. (1988). Preservice teacher training—Promoting effective teachers. In L. H. Golubchick & B. Persky (Eds.), *Urban, social, and educational issues* (pp. 150–155). Garden City, NY: Avery.

Purpel, D. (1989). *The moral and spiritual crisis in education: A curriculum for justice and compassion in education.* Granby, MA: Bergin & Garvey.

Rallis, S. F. (1990). Professional teachers and restructured schools: Leadership challenges. In B. Mitchell & L. Cunningham (Eds.), *Educational leadership and changing contexts of families, communities, and schools: Eighty-ninth yearbook of the National Society for the Study of Education* (pp. 184–209). Chicago: University of Chicago Press.

Report of the Surgeon General's workshop on children with HIV *infection.* (1986). Washington, DC: U.S. Department of Health & Human Services.

Rich, J. M. (1971). *Education and human values.* Reading, MA: Addison-Wesley.

Rose, M. (1989). *Lives on the boundary: A moving account of the struggles and achievements of America's educational underclass.* New York: Penguin.

Rosenholtz, S. J., & Simpson, C. (1990). Workplace conditions and the rise and fall of teachers' commitment. *Sociology of Education, 63,* 241–257.

Rudder, C. F. (1991). Ethics and educational administration: Are ethical policies "ethical"? *Educational Theory, 41*(1), 75–88.

Rutter, M., Maughan, B., Mortimore, P., Ouston, J., & Smith, A. (1979). *Fifteen thousand hours.* Cambridge, MA: Harvard University Press.

Salinger, J. D. (1951). *The catcher in the rye.* New York: Bantam.

Scales, P. (1983). Adolescent sexuality and education: Principles, approaches, and resources. In C. Chilman (Ed.), *Adolescent sexuality in a changing American society* (pp. 207–229). New York: Wiley.

Scarr, S. (1985). Constructing psychology: Making facts and fables for our times. *American Psychologist, 40,* 499–512.

Schaps, E., & Solomon, D. (1990). Schools and classrooms as caring communities. *Educational Leadership, 48*(3), 38–42.

Schlechty, P. C. (1989). Career ladders: A good idea going awry. In T. J. Sergiovanni & J. H. Moore (Eds.), *Schooling for tomorrow: Directing reform to issues that count* (pp. 356–374). Boston: Allyn & Bacon.

Schmuck, P. (Ed.). (1987). *Women educators: Employees of schools in western countries.* Albany: State University of New York Press.

Schmuck, R. A., & Schmuck, P. A. (1988). *Group processes in the classroom* (5th ed.). Douglas, IA: Wm. C. Brown.

Schön, D. A. (1983). *The reflective practitioner: How professionals think in action.* New York: Basic.

Schön, D. A. (1984). Leadership as reflection-in-action. In T. J. Sergiovanni & J. E. Corbally (Eds.), *Leadership and organizational culture: New perspectives on administrative theory and practice* (pp. 36–63). Urbana: University of Illinois Press.

Schön, D. A. (1987). *Educating the reflective practitioner: Toward a new design for thinking and learning in the professions.* San Francisco: Jossey-Bass.

Schorr, L. (1989). *Within our reach: Breaking the cycle of disadvantage.* New York: Doubleday.

Schubert, W. H. (1991). Teacher love: A basis for understanding praxis. In C. Witherell & N. Noddings (Eds.), *Stories lives tell: Narrative and dialogue in education* (pp. 207–233). New York: Teachers College Press.

Schumacher, E. F. (1977). *A guide for the perplexed.* New York: Harper & Row.

Sedlak, M. W., Wheeler, C. W., Pullin, D. C., & Cusick, P. A. (1986). *Selling students short: Classroom bargains and academic reform in the American high school.* New York: Teachers College Press.

Sergiovanni, T. J. (1980, Winter). A social humanities view of educational policy and administration. *Educational Administration Quarterly, 16*(1), 1–19.

Sergiovanni, T. J. (1984). Developing a relevant theory of administration. In T. J. Sergiovanni & J. E. Corbally (Eds.), *Leadership and organizational culture: New perspec-*

tives on administrative theory and practice (pp. 275–292). Urbana: University of Illinois Press.

Sergiovanni, T. J. (1987). *The principalship: A reflective practice perspective.* Boston: Allyn & Bacon.

Sergiovanni, T. J. (1989). What really counts in improving schools? In T. J. Sergiovanni & J. H. Moore (Eds.), *Schooling for tomorrow: Directing reform to issues that count* (pp. 1–8). Boston: Allyn & Bacon.

Sergiovanni, T. J. (1992). *Moral leadership: Getting to the heart of school improvement.* San Francisco: Jossey-Bass.

Sergiovanni, T. J., & Starratt, R. J. (1988). *Supervision: Human perspectives.* New York: McGraw-Hill.

Shakeshaft, C. (1987). *Women in educational administration.* Newbury Park, CA: Sage.

Shea, C. M. (1990). Pentagon vs. multinational capitalism: The political economy of the 1980s school reform movement. In C. M. Shea, E. Kahane, & P. Sola (Eds.), *The new servants of power: A critique of the 1980s school reform movement* (pp. 3–38). New York: Praeger.

Shea, C. M., Kahane, E., & Sola, P. (Eds.). (1990). *The new servants of power: A critique of the 1980s school reform movement.* New York: Praeger.

Sheehy, G. (1977). *Passages: Predictable crises of adult life.* New York: Dutton.

Shelley, M. (1981). *Frankenstein.* New York: Bantam. (Original work published 1818)

Shulman, L. S. (1989). Teaching alone, learning together: Needed agendas for the new reforms. In T. J. Sergiovanni & J. H. Moore (Eds.), *Schooling for tomorrow: Directing reforms to issues that count* (pp. 186–187). Boston: Allyn & Bacon.

Silberman, C. E. (1970). *Crisis in the classroom.* New York: Random House.

Sizer, T. R. (1985). *Horace's compromises: The dilemma of the American high school.* Boston: Houghton Mifflin.

Slavin, R. E. (1980). Cooperative learning. *Review of Educational Research, 50,* 315–342.

Slavin, R. E. (1983). *Cooperative learning.* New York: Longman.

Slavin, R. E., & Madden, N. A. (1989, February). What works for students at risk: A research synthesis. *Educational Leadership, 46,* 4–13.

Smith, K. L., & Zepp, I. G. (1974). *Search for the beloved community: The thinking of Martin Luther King.* Valley Forge, PA: Judson.

Smith, P. (1990). *Killing the spirit: Higher education in America.* New York: Viking.

Snyder, K. J. (1983). Instructional leadership for productive schools. *Educational Leadership,* 32–37.

Springsted, E. (1988). *Who will make us wise?* Cambridge, MA: Cowley.

Starratt, R. J. (1991). Building an ethical school: A theory for practice in educational leadership. *Educational Administration Quarterly, 27*(2), 185–202.

Stout, J. (1988). *Ethics after Babel: The languages of morals and their discontents.* Boston: Beacon.

Strike, K. A. (1982). *Educational policy and the just society.* Chicago: University of Illinois Press.

Strike, K., Haller, E., & Soltis, J. (1988). *The ethics of educational administration.* New York: Teachers College Press.

Taylor, C. (1989). *Sources of the self.* Cambridge, MA: Harvard University Press.

Taylor, F. W. (1911). *The principles of scientific management.* New York: Harper & Row.

Thomas, B. R. (1990). The school as a moral learning community. In J. Goodlad, R. Soder, & K. A. Sirotnik (Eds.), *The moral dimensions of teaching* (pp. 266–295). San Francisco: Jossey-Bass.

Thompson, J. D. (1956). Authority and power in "identical" organizations. *American Journal of Sociology, 62,* 290–301.

Toch, T. (1991). *In the name of excellence: The struggle to reform the nation's schools, why it's failing, and what should be done.* New York: Oxford University Press.

Treisman, P. M. (1986). *A study of mathematics performance of black students at the University of California, Berkeley.* Unpublished dissertation, University of California, Berkeley.

Twain, M. (1981). *The adventures of Huckleberry Finn.* New York: Bantam. (Original work published 1885)

Tyack, D., & Hansot, E. (1982). *Managers of virtue: Public school leadership in America, 1820–1980.* New York: Basic.

United States Department of Education. (1984). *The nation responds: Recent efforts to improve education.* Washington, DC: Author.

United States Department of Education. (1987). *AIDS and the education of our children: A guide for parents and teachers.* Washington, DC: Author.

United States Department of Education. (1989). *The nation responds: Recent efforts to improve education.* Washington, DC: Author.

Vaill, P. B. (1984). The purposing of high-performing systems. In T. J. Sergiovanni & J. E. Corbally (Eds.), *Leadership and organizational culture: New perspectives on administrative theory and practice* (pp. 85–104). Urbana: University of Illinois Press.

Vinovskis, M. (1988). *An "epidemic" of adolescent pregnancy? Some historical and political considerations.* New York: Oxford University Press.

Wagstaff, L. H., & Gallagher, K. S. (1990). Schools, families, and communities: Idealized images and new realities. In B. Mitchell & L. Cunningham (Eds.), *Educational leadership and changing contexts of families, communities and schools: Eighty-ninth yearbook for the National Society for the Study of Education* (pp. 91–117). Chicago: University of Chicago Press.

Watson, D. (1980). *Caring for strangers.* London: Routledge & Kegan Paul.

Weber, M. (1947). *The theory of social and economic organization* (T. Parsons, Trans.). New York: Free Press.

Weinstein, F. (1989). Health educators: Where are you? *Health Education, 19*(16) 21–22.

Weinstein, R. S. (1983). Student perceptions of schooling. *Elementary School Journal, 83*(4), 287–312.

Wilshire, B. (1990). *The moral collapse of the American university: Professionalism, purity, and alienation.* Albany: State University of New York Press.

Wilson, R. (1987). Bennett calls character training, not new federal programs, key to competitiveness. *Education Week,* p. 29.

Wise, A. E. (1989). Professional teaching: A new paradigm for the management of education. In T. J. Sergiovanni and J. H. Moore (Eds.), *Schooling for tomor-*

row: Directing reforms to issues that count (pp. 301–310). Boston: Allyn & Bacon.

Witherell, C., & Noddings, N. (Eds.). (1991). *Stories lives tell: Narrative and dialogue in education.* New York: Teachers College Press.

Wittrock, M. (Ed.). (1986). *Handbook of research on teaching.* New York: Macmillan.

Young, M. (1989–1990). Characteristics of high potential and at-risk teachers. *Action in Teacher Education, 11*(4), 35–40.

Zirkel, P. A., & MacMurtrie, F. L. (1988). Supreme court decisions affecting education. In L. H. Golubchick & B. Persky (Eds.), *Urban, social, and educational issues* (pp.18–23). Garden City, NY: Avery.

Index

About the Author

Lynn G. Beck, assistant professor of education at the University of California, Los Angeles, received her Ph.D. from Vanderbilt University. Her research and teaching interests include the ethics of educational administration, the principalship, and administrator preparation. Recent publications include *Understanding the Principalship: Metaphorical Themes, 1920s–1990s* (1993) and *Ethical Dimensions of Administrator Preparation Programs* (forthcoming) (both with Joseph Murphy) and "Meeting Future Challenges: The Place of a Caring Ethic in Educational Administration" (1992).